THE WINDS OF HOPE FOR A WORLD OUT OF BREATH

A Study Of The
23rd Psalm

BY ROBERT G. TUTTLE

C.S.S. Publishing Co., Inc.
Lima, Ohio

THE WINDS OF HOPE FOR A WORLD OUT OF BREATH

Copyright © 1993 by
The C.S.S. Publishing Company, Inc.
Lima, Ohio

All rights reserved. No part of this publication may be reproduced, stored in a retrieval system, or transmitted in any form or by any means, electronic, mechanical, photocopying, recording, or otherwise, without the prior permission of the publisher. Inquiries should be addressed to: The C.S.S. Publishing Company, Inc., 628 South Main Street, Lima, Ohio 45804.

Scripture Quotations are from the *King James Version of the Bible*, in the public domain.

Library of Congress Cataloging-in-Publication Data

Tuttle, Robert G., 1907-
  The winds of hope for a world out of breath: a study of the 23rd Psalm / by Robert G. Tuttle.
    97 p. 14 by 21.5 cm.
  ISBN 1-55673-508-1
  1. Bible. O.T. Psalms XXIII—Meditations. I. Title.
BS1450 23rd.T78 1993
223'.206—dc20   92-31682
                                                                  CIP

9300 / ISBN 1-55673-508-1   PRINTED IN U.S.A.

To my mother,
Janie Gregory Tuttle,
who taught me the Bible.

Table Of Contents

	Introduction	7
	The Shepherd God	11
I.	The Still	19
II.	What Do You Mean — He Restoreth My Soul?	31
IV.	A Straight Path In A Crooked World	39
V.	Finding God In The Narrows Of Life	49
VI.	Sustained In Time Of Difficulty	59
VII.	God's Extravagance	71
VIII.	The Final Dimensions Of Life	79
IX.	The Shepherd God Comes To Earth	87

Introduction

This is a study of the 23rd Psalm and speaks to our daily exhaustion. So often in our daily contacts we hear the sigh "I am so tired." Constantly in my counseling, I feel the burden carried by those who come to me for help.

Guilt, fear, hate, stress, loneliness, sickness all go to make up the burden that we bear, and alone, it is a burden too heavy to be borne. The 23rd Psalm opens a door to guidance and help.

Burn-out is a modern term for fatigue: "I am so tired." But there is a wind of faith and trust and hope that blows through the entire 23rd Psalm. God touches us with his love and restores our soul. There is the goodness and mercy; there is the house of the Lord forever.

This book is a devotional study of the 23rd Psalm. It speaks to the world in stress. The Psalmist brings us to a calmer, more creative acceptance of life.

The book will be helpful for personal devotional reading, for study groups, and for a background of preaching on the 23rd Psalm.

Psalm 23

The Lord *is* my shepherd; I shall not want.

He maketh me to lie down in green pastures:
    he leadeth me beside the still waters.

He restoreth my soul: he leadeth me in the
    paths of righteousoness for his name's sake.

Yea, though I walk through the valley of the
    shadow of death, I will fear no evil;
    for thou *art* with me; thy rod and thy
    staff they comfort me.

Thou preparest a table before me in the presence
    of mine enemies; thou anointest my head with oil;
    my cup runneth over.

Surely goodness and mercy shall follow me all the
    days of my life; and I will dwell in the house of
    the Lord for ever.

CHAPTER I
The Shepherd God

> *"The Lord is my Shepherd*
> *I shall not want."*
> Psalm 23:1

There is the ancient spring of Air Farah lying northeast of Jerusalem. This is generally accepted as the scene of David's boyhood. The youngest son of the Hebrew family was the one who kept the sheep. This beautiful spot in the wilderness fits the atmosphere of the Twenty-third Psalm. It was probably there that the prophet anointed the boy, David, King of Israel.

The authorship of the 23rd Psalm is not absolutely certain, but it could fit well into David's mature years. After his youthful sin with Bathsheba, after his repentance, his forgiveness and his restoration by God, David became a beautiful soul — "A man after God's own heart." We like to think of David writing this psalm after he had passed through the struggles of life, and in it all, had discovered a deep and abiding faith in God. So now his soul declares the beauty and depth of his confident trust in the Shepherd God. Perhaps, too, we can discover this faith in the wilderness pilgrimage of our own living.

A little girl misquoted this verse:

> *"The Lord is my shepherd,*
> *That's all I want."*

Not bad!

"Man has put himself on the throne of the Universe; but the universe has pulled the throne out from under him." The Universe knows who is in control:

"The Lord is my shepherd."

In a technological age, technology alone, out of control, threatens us with death. We must rediscover the universe that cares so that we may care. We cry out for a faith great enough, a love deep enough to redeem this age.

God has not surrendered to technology. He designed it and empowered it to be servant — not master. Science is not God, but God's instrument. The test tube is not ultimate reality. People cannot be savior to their own lostness. In spite of our sophistication and scientific independence we are still "wanting." I am spiritually hungry. Back of all this, "The Lord is my Shepherd." The universe really cares. I shall not want for any necessary thing. With God alive, we are never helpless.

Grace Kelly, when she was eight years old, wrote a little verse that expresses a basic fear:

> *"I hate to see the sun go down,*
> *And squeeze itself into the ground;*
> *For fear some time it might get stuck,*
> *And then tomorrow not come up."*

But God is in charge, and it does come up.

The sad truth is: "We have built us a monumental world. We have slaved for it; have spent upon the outside all that is of value within our nature — while inside, our world is left shabby and insufficient." "Humankind," Bergson suggests, "lies groaning half crushed beneath the weight of his own progress — his soul too small to fill it; too weak to guide it." Our secular, materialistic life forces us to agree: "The technological body, now larger, calls for a bigger soul; but we have sold our soul for the body and have no soul — we are dead!" Yes, without a greater living faith, we are doomed. God is still alive and near; but we are not aware.

We have been looking "downstream" for life's meaning; when meaning is to be found "upstream." In our accelerating economy, we awake at 3 o'clock in the morning all full of anxieties, full of hunger and fears, realizing that the deep-freeze is full, but that there is not enough spiritual food in the house to last out the night.

We are still in want, even in the abundance of a technological age. It would make us less desperate, less dangerous, to know in our hearts that God cares, really cares. He is infinitely more powerful and more loving than we have ever imagined. He is like Jesus: "absolute authority; total compassion."

> *"He shall feed his flock like a shepherd;*
> *He shall gather the lambs with his arm,*
> *And shall carry them in his bosom,*
> *And shall gently lead those that are with young."*
> Isaiah 40:11

That means something to me. That fills the spiritual vacuum. God is not an arbitrary, "dice-throwing God." "The Lord is my shepherd." The Shepherd knows his sheep by name. The sheep know his voice. When we really believe this, and respond to it, it will change the climate of the world.

"Our God is too small." You can't play around with God and keep your sanity. We can't play along with shallow theologians saying, "God is dead;" nor with a flighty movie actress declaring, "God is a perfect doll;" nor with many unthinking people glibly saying, "The person upstairs." God is God All Mighty, designer, creator, sustainer of the universe. I still believe that the God of Creation who designed the progressing miracle of evolution; the God of Moses and the emerging nations; the God of Christ involved with and suffering with his people, is big enough and practical enough to cope with the technological age, to bring it into line, and to fill it with meaningful life. Listen:

> *"He that dwelleth in the secret place of the most High shall abide under the shadow of the Almighty.*
> *. . . He is my refuge and my fortress: my God; in him will I trust . . .*
> *He shall cover thee with his feathers, and under his wings shall thou trust.*
> *Thou shalt not be afraid for the terror by night, nor for the arrow that flieth by day;*
> *Nor for the pestilence that walketh in darkness; nor for the destruction that wasteth at noonday."*
> Psalm 91:1-6

Life has teeth in it, sometimes sharp teeth. Faith must be rugged enough to cope with life as it is. "The Lord is my Shepherd," just might be the answer to the dreadful vacuum at the heart of this secular age — the age that raises questions and does not answer them.

In this time when often marriage vows are not taken seriously, when children are neglected and abused, when too many young adults still carry the scars of not having been loved in their childhood, the rediscovery of the God who is like Jesus could give us peace and put us back on track again. Isn't it possible for us to see that when we have repudiated Christ in our thinking and in our living, that "real life has already deserted us and our world itself is moving in a kind of ritual dance toward death?" The death of the bomb, or the slower, surer death of rottenness.

In all of this the Shepherd God pursues us in love — even through the ravines, the thorns, the brambles, the desert stones of today's world. Even the bad people are his people. But the loving "Hound of Heaven" is out looking for us all night long when we are lost. But we run away from his love and hide behind our sins and selfishness. And that is the end of the road.

"The soul of each person is under the siege of God (Douglas Steere)" who calls, "Come in, come in, come all the way in." But we stumble along, half in and half out of life, willing to pray on one knee, but afraid to put both knees down. "The great effective act of faith is when a person decides that he is not God," and surrenders to ultimate love and eternal life.

But so much of God's healing love is hidden deep in life and we take it for granted. For example, if you fly to La Paz, Bolivia, and land there on the Alta Plain at 13,000 feet altitude, as you disembark from the plane you will feel weak and sick, and possibly faint. After about two weeks you will feel alright. What has happened? Without your knowing it, God (through nature) has doubled or quadrupled your red blood corpuscles so that now they can carry sufficient oxygen to your oxygen hungry cells. You have been mysteriously sustained by the Shepherd God.

The psalmist knew this:

> The Lord shall preserve thee from all evil: he shall preserve thy soul.
> The Lord shall preserve thy going out and thy coming in from this time forth, and even for evermore.
> The Lord is thy keeper . . .
> . . . he that keepeth thee will not slumber.
> Behold, he that keepeth (thee) shall neither slumber nor sleep.
>
> (Psalm 121 — Selected verses)

Someone wisely suggests that the "universal concern" of God ought to make us a "people of universal concern." And that is what a Christian is: a caring person, living in a realm of caring people, under a caring God. Each caring for everybody else, and therefore each being cared for.

While we are so deeply obsessed by "self-protection" and "self promotion," we cancel out the universal concern which could bring us the experience of self-fulfillment instead of the devastating selfishness that now strangles us. If we really know the Shepherd God we can no longer think in terms of a "satisfactory kill-ratio" in our dealings with our enemies. Instead our national passion would be an authentic motivation toward peace. I like these words from an editorial in *The Christian Century:*

> *'God is love.' Sometimes punishing, sometimes rewarding us, but always loving us. Whether he is calling us down or lifting us up, God loves us. God doesn't give us up even when we stumble. He sticks.*

When I am convinced, both consciously and subconsciously, that "the Lord is my Shepherd," then I have an authentic motivation both for life and for peace.

The Shepherd God is shepherding us, and through us shepherding others. An excellent surgeon left my church and a good practice to go as a medical missionary to Pakistan. He wrote me about a little girl with a dangerously inactive kidney whose life he had saved through a delicate surgical procedure.

She had no money; she would have died; but her life was saved by the Shepherd God who had called a Christian doctor to serve where things were most difficult and unrewarding. The doctor, however, was overjoyed at the door God had opened to him, and at the life he had saved. God works through Christ; Christ works through Christians.

The Shepherd is at work in many ways: It is the Shepherd instinct in us that cares for our children; it is the Shepherd spirit in the doctor that cares for his patients; it is the Shepherd spirit that makes us care for those who work for us and those who work with us — and those whose paths we cross every day.

But how could humanity have strayed so badly if the Lord is our Shepherd? The Shepherd does not push the sheep; he leads them. Some will not follow. Some are so self-involved they cannot see him nor hear his call. Some of us are "so broadminded that we are flat-headed." We are smothering ourselves in our own embrace. We do not want what God wants. We are afraid of the Shepherd because he carries a cross; and that is a threat to our comfortable living. But let it not be forgotten, it is with that cross of caring that he saves us. It is with that cross that he sends us out to save others.

The Shepherd God stands in the midst of life's wilderness; in the dangerous terrain of life, where the rocks and the ravines threaten; where the wolves roam; where the refreshing springs are hard to find. God meets us where the problem is. Life is a fact! Death is a fact! Sorrow and pain and joy are facts. This Existential world is the place where things come to pass! Events continually invade our lives. With all our technical perfection, cars pile up on our highways, our loved ones may be involved; planes collide and dive into crowds of people; ships ram each other at sea; disease and death attack mansion and hut alike. There is no real assurance in our brilliant technology. Will the next launch into space be consumed by fire? Will the ejector eject? Will someone drop the bomb? Our lives are invaded again and again by joy and by sorrow; by despair and by hope. There has to be something beyond the physical. All this does not deny God. It is in the event we meet God, and walk with him beyond the event.

There is something more. Under the growl of the atom, in a world held hostage, amidst the fragments of our broken homes, our broken lives, in the concerns of our confused youth, with us in our desperate need, stands the Shepherd God. The Shepherd on a cross! This is another kind of event; it happened; they crucified him. Life was rough on him — the kind of life we have to face. Jesus was hurt and he understands our hurt.

But there is still another event — the resurrection. The bonds of death are forever broken! The Good Shepherd was destroyed. And yet he came back and gathered his disciples into a working unit of effective love — filled with his spirit. The resurrection, the event to answer all other events! "Nothing can separate us from the love of Christ!" "In the world you shall have tribulation — but I have overcome the world." Christ is the ultimate reality. This is not naive thinking, but a simple statement of fact. By faith, the Christian discovers here a basis for a life of great and confident living in any age.

Dr. George Buttrick suggests that people think that they have waited and waited for a God who never comes, for a God who makes promises and does not fulfill them — God does come! God came and they did not know him when he came. He is at the door and knocking, now. But we are listening to television!

The word, the event, the shepherd "are new in every new age. The gift from God who gives new songs in every new night — who leads God's human flock by mountains and desert, by storm and sunlight of this world, to a New City!"

*"The Lord is my shepherd;
I shall not want."*

In God do I put my trust.

CHAPTER II
The Still

*"He maketh me to lie down in green pastures
He leadeth me beside the still waters."*
                                    Psalm 23:2

The Interpreter's Bible supports the sequence here. Early in the morning while the dew is still on the grass the shepherd wakes the sheep. He leads them forth toward the pasture lands. Perhaps the first stage of the journey is over a small mountain. Soon they are going down the other side toward a quietly flowing stream. The shepherd makes the sheep stop for a short rest. While they rest they can drink from the stream and nibble at the rich succulent grass. They are refreshed and are ready to move on, always led by the shepherd who is thinking of their welfare.

For persons of faith, that is the picture of life. The poor fellow who griped: "Life is just one darn thing after another," didn't know about the green pastures and the still waters. Nor did he know the Shepherd. God wants to give us fulfillment and peace; we demand abundance.

Someone pictures the stages of getting on in the world:
Stage one — one car.
Stage two — two cars.
Stage three — a swimming pool in the garden.
Stage four — an island in the pool to get away from it all.
There are so many lines of fracture in our living.

There is need for the green pastures and the still waters. With a note of nostalgia John Quinn states the case:

Front Porches
*NOBODY sits on porches any more
Of summer evenings heady with the scent
Of four-o'clocks and damp petunias,*

> *Rocks in the creaking silence while the soft*
> *Murmur of robins dwindles into dusk.*
> *That interlude before the gathering night*
> *Has set like junket, now is obsolete.*
> *Ambitious men have not the patience nor the time,*
> *To rest the heels of their world upon a rail.*
> (John Robert Quinn)

On the other hand two Scott Fitzgerald characters paint the picture of contemporary boredom:

> *"What will we do with ourselves this afternoon?"*
> *Daisy answers:*
> *"What will we do with ourselves tomorrow,*
>   *And the day after that,*
>   *And the next 30 years?"*

In our weariness and our frustration we need the old hymn:

> *"Art thou weary?*
>   *Art thou troubled?*
>   *Art thou sore distressed?*
>   *There's One to whom we come,*
>   *And coming find our rest."*

The Lord is our Shepherd. The green pastures and the still waters are real.

There is a custom in the British Navy, writes Margaret Blair Johnstone, that when a crisis occurs on a fighting vessel — explosion, fire, torpedo, bomb — the "Still" is blown. What does this mean? Every British fighting man knows. It means "Stop! Freeze! Do nothing! Do not panic! Prepare to do the wise thing! Calculate your position! Check your resources! Consider the wisest course of action!" Following this course of action, many lives have been saved, and many ships have come through.

This speaks to our breathless technological age. "Be still and know." Don't push the panic button. "Be still and know." There is a shepherding, providing, caring God — there are still waters and green pastures along the way.

In the contemporary crisis God is speaking; he is calling for the "Still:"

> *Stop, pause, do nothing, appraise the situation, check your resources, determine the wisest course of action.*

Have a rendezvous with God. Have a tryst with truth. Life demands it. This goes for my personal life, my home, my business, my nation, my world. We are rushing headlong into dangerous involvements.

One frustrated fellow in Brooklyn rushed out of his front door and punched a passerby on the nose. In court he testified that he had had a quarrel with his wife. Instead of punching her, he had the bad luck to punch a police detective. The "still" would have saved him a lot of trouble.

Verses from another Psalm point the way:

> *"Before the mountains were brought forth,*
> *or ever thou hadst founded*
> *the earth and the world,*
> *Even from everlasting to everlasting*
> *Thou art God . . .*
> *For a thousand years in thy sight*
> *Are as but yesterday when it is past,*
> *And as a watch in the night . . .*
> *Let thy work appear unto thy servants,*
> *And thy glory unto thy children.*
> *And let the beauty of the Lord*
> *Our God be upon us;*
> *And establish thou the work*
> *Of our hands upon us:*
> *Yea, the work of our hands*
> *Establish thou it!"*
>
> (Psalm 90 — Selected verses)

This puts life in perspective.

There is one clear explanation of our frustration and our exhaustion. We haven't found our way as persons in the New Age. For about 6,000 years our ancestors lived a fairly steady life. Things didn't change drastically. The pattern of life remained about the same. It was mainly an agricultural, small town type of life. There was the farm, and simple business. There were plants and animals. The family — parents and children — worked together. It was a simple life. The church and the school were at the center of life.

Suddenly, when I was a child a new world broke in upon us. Great industries began to gobble up the members of the family. No longer did family members work as a group. Then mothers started to work away from home. Close ties with the children were lost. Movies and television took over. Automobiles, airplanes, space ships carried us around at great speeds. Life became a combination of sound and speed. Children no longer had the fun of making their toys. Drugs and alcohol became a way of life.

Humanity cannot absorb a new age in one generation. Our fathers and mothers and our grandparents, through several thousand years, had learned to be at home in the old pattern of life. We have not yet learned how to handle the New World with all its pressures. We are not going back to the Old World; we must develop a rich quality of life in the New World. But how?

Long ago God blew the "Still:" "Be still and know that I am God." Check out your resources; they are a gift from God. Your physical energies, your spiritual energies are sufficient for the modern world. God is full of surprises. Even the pressures of the New Age and our desperation can drive us back to Faith. We are forced to re-think life. The Christian is the key person for the New Age. By faith he is oriented in the wisdom of the past and the assurance of the future. The Christian is at home in the Forever.

William Wordsworth had this insight into the depths of life:

Sweet Recess
"We scaled without a track
to ease our steps,
A steep ascent; and reached
a dreary plane,
With a tumultuous waste
of huge hill tops

Before us; savage region!
    Which I paced
Dispirited: when all at once,
    behold!
Beneath our feet a little lonely vale.
A lowly vale, and yet uplifted high
Among the mountains; even as if
    the spot
Had been from eldest time by
    wish of theirs
So placed, to be shut out from
    All the world!
Urnlike it was in shape, deep
    as an urn;
With rocks encompassed, save
    that to the South
Was one small opening, where
    a heath-clad ridge
Supplied a boundary less abrupt
    and close;
A quiet treeless rook, with
    two green fields,
A liquid pool that glittered
    in the sun,
And one bare dwelling; one
    abode, no more!
It seemed the home of poverty
    and toil,
Though not of want: the little
    field made green
By husbandry of many thrifty years,
Paid cheerful tribute to the
    moorland house . . . .
Ah! What a sweet recess thought
    I, is here!
Instantly throwing down my
    limbs at ease
Upon a bed of heath . . .
How tenderly protected! Far and near
We have an image of the pristine earth . . ."

There are so many ways to find sanctuary, to break the tension, to renew the spirit. But too often we have ears and do not hear; eyes and do not see. Even the disciples had difficulty comprehending. Jesus had to prod their understanding: "Philip, Philip, after all this time, after all this time, and you don't know me." The Psalmist had to refresh the memory of his people: "Before the mountains were brought forth, or even thou hadst formed the earth and the world, even from everlasting to everlasting, thou art God (Psalm 90:2)." This we must know, e're we find ourselves.

Once, in a strange way, I stumbled into peace. The soul must find sanctuary: God requires it; life demands it. I was flying with a bush pilot in Alaska, and I noticed that we were running out of gas. We were flying over the wilderness down near Mount McKinley. The pilot didn't seem to be bothered but I was. I asked, "What are we going to do — you can't buy that stuff down here." His reply: "I'm glad we're running out of gas, because I want to show you the most beautiful lake in the world." With that he turned the little plane toward the sheer granite cliffs and icy glaciers of Mount McKinley. I didn't see how anyone could hang a lake up there against those cliffs and glaciers. Suddenly, we broke through a ravine, and there it was. A bit of sapphire three miles long and three-quarters of a mile wide, surrounded by tundra, banks of snow, silence and towering mountains. Maneuvering a difficult turn, he put the plane down at the end of the lake. We taxied to the other end, surrounded by beaver hutches and leaping mountain trout. I saw his face fall — his camp had been raided by a grizzly bear. His tent was torn to shreds; his rubber boat had been destroyed; all his cans of food had been crushed and sucked dry of their contents. The one thing that saved us was that the old bear did not like the smell of gasoline, so the cans of gasoline had been untouched. There was no trail to the lake. It was lost in beauty and complete quietness — a sanctuary! Every now and then when I am about to suffer burn-out; my soul goes back to this spot and I am refreshed and restored.

We don't have to continue stumbling around with our heads down, crushed by fear, worry, guilt and hate. Our Heavenly Father wants us to be free. He will forgive us, empower us, put us on our feet and keep us there. True prayer is the key. Once I was enjoying lunch at Belmont Abbey, sitting next to one of their priest-teachers. I believe that he was a biology professor and football coach. I asked, "How much time each day do you spend in prayer and meditation?" His answer surprised me, "I spend two and a half hours each morning." The failure to spend serious blocks of time in prayer may be the point at which we Protestants are failing.

We might not spend 2½ hours each day. But it would make a tremendous difference if we would only spend 15 to 20 minutes each day in Bible reading, prayer and meditation — thinking with God on the issues and values of life and receiving from him understanding, courage, hope, joy and peace. Our world needs people who are in touch with the ultimate things of life, and still in touch with people. "Be still and know." If we don't have time, we do not have time for life. At times "He maketh me to lie down (illness, exhaustion, accident, burn-out)," because he loves me.

A friend of mine, Dr. William Wilson, formerly of Duke Medical School, found his breakthrough into new life observing a beautiful sunset during a canoe cruise in the wilderness of Canada. Some find sanctuary in good music, some by relaxing in a tub of hot water. When we served a church deep in the mountains of western North Carolina and our children were small, my wife Lillian would find her peace looking out over the kitchen sink at Black Rock, a peak high in the Balsam Mountains. A doctor in our church in Statesville would come by the church at 2 a.m., returning from surgery at the hospital. He would kneel at the altar of a little chapel that we kept open and lit all night long. There he would receive quietness, peace and power through a definite sense of the presence of God. He had patience and strength others did not understand.

Once I knelt where Jesus knelt on the shore of Galilee and prayed as I watched the sun rise over the Syrian hills. As the sun lightened the dark landscape I could hear and understand the phrase of the Lord's Prayer: "For thine is the kingdom and the power and the glory, forever, and forever, Amen." I was renewed; and am renewed again and again by the memory. All these are experiences of the "Still:" stop, freeze, appraise the situation, review your resources, contemplate the wise course of action. Gaze upon the mind of God!

In these days the family, as a unit, needs the experience of the green pastures and the still waters. When our three children were small the family spent a month in a little cabin 9,000 feet up in the Rocky Mountains. We picked huckleberries and Lillian made huckleberry pies. We caught beautiful rainbow trout in high mountain streams. Robert told his mother: "I caught three trout 9,000 feet high." Our black Labrador spent the month chasing chipmunks in the yard.

One day the three children and I walked 11 miles up beyond the tree level to a little lake 12,000 feet high. The sheer precipice of Long's Peak rose from this lake to 15,000 feet, touching the sky above us. A little stream gurgled through the grass as the grass gently swayed in the breeze. We could glimpse spots of the old world far below. We were translated into a new world of peace and freedom. Here, as a family, we unconsciously learned how to appreciate each other, to forgive, to be helpful, to grow, to catch distant visions, to be joyful and aware of our everlasting future.

Especially, in the tensions of today do husbands and wives need the quietness of green pastures and still waters. In order to enrich their relationships, to deepen their understanding of each other, to release new experiences of at-oneness and mutual joy with each other, they should slip away for a week or a weekend alone, together in some enchanting spot. But some husbands and wives are afraid to look into the reflections that are revealed in the deep, quiet pools of thought and self-examination. They do not want to admit their faults, their anxieties and their resentments. Their surface lives are turbulent, because the inner person is struggling with frustrations and doubts. These husbands and wives need to visit the green pastures and the still waters together, that they might discover themselves in depth, and rediscover each other in love. It is possible for love to be renewed. Walking hand in hand through the mystic paths of Brook Green Gardens near Myrtle Beach, or strolling together over the trails of Joyce Kilmer Forest in western North Carolina, can fan into flame the old mysterious feelings of tenderness, once so vivid and exciting.

But, sadly, the contemporary spirit is to hurry about everything. Since we do not know how to cope with new ways of life, we rush on, afraid to stop and face it. We rush on our vacation; we rush to get home. We even rock a rocking chair at dangerous speeds. We hurry to rest, but are too exhausted and uptight to find repose. No wonder we burn-out. "The mind diseased;" "the rooted sorrow;" "the written troubles of the brain;" "that terrible stuff that weighs upon the heart." Shakespeare drew an accurate picture of our tensions.

Thomas Kelley suggests a point of hope, even in this kind of world:

> *"Deep within us all there is an*
>   *Amazing inner sanctuary of the soul;*
> *A holy place, a Divine Center,*
>   *A speaking source,*
> *To which we continually return.*
> *Eternity is at our hearts,*
>   *Pressing upon our time-worn lives,*
> *Warning us with an intimation*
>   *of an astounding destiny,*
> *Calling us home into itself."*

Don't give up! Green pastures and still waters are real; and God is there! And Jesus meant it when he pleaded:

> *"Come unto me*
> *All ye who labor*
> *And are heavy laden;*
> *And I will give you rest."*
>   (Matthew 11:28)

"Fear not; be not afraid," is still his message of assurance.

In his hour of trail Jesus went to his own green pasture, the garden of Gethsemane. Kneeling at a stone under an ancient olive tree the Master prayed, sweating as it were drops of blood. He saw, even then, the shadow of the cross. He was not crushed, but prayed, "Thy will, not mine, be done." He saw, through God's eyes, that his death would be the instrument of the world's redemption, he was at peace. He marched through the terrible events of the next day with calm, and Divine dignity. He saved a poor sinner on the next cross, and cried out in agony, yet eternal assurance: "Into thy hands I commend my spirit." And then the resurrection! The green pastures "will put foundations under our feet and a sky of high visibility above our heads." This is not an escape from reality; but an escape into reality. It is moving with the Shepherd from the crushing facts of surface life, into the unlimited healing experiences of the depths of life.

It was even in the wilderness that Jesus had discovered the meaning of his Messiahship — not bread, not show, not military power — but people and love and healing and eternal life. Jesus loved the Sea of Galilee, the barren hills surrounding it, even the quiet darkness of the early morning. There the Father ministered to him.

Like Jesus, from the green pastures we can emerge into effective action. We have time to spare, because God has time to spare for us, and we emerge into a new sanity. By still waters, we see the Hell of life for what it is. We learn to hate stupidity — even our own stupidity. With clearer vision we turn to God. We see life "soul-sized." But too many of us are "God Evaders." We rush from one frustrating responsibility to another, and fail to stop at the places of renewal. Green pastures are not just for the licking of our wounds; green pastures are for the feeding of our souls. Even in the toughest encounters of life, we are not far from the still waters. God can be found in strange places.

What if we do have a Shepherd God? What if there is love at the heart of the universe? And we do not have time to realize it, nor faith to live by it? But perish, even when life is available? This is the sorrow of God! This is the cross of Christ!

It's just as simple as this: We perish under the demands of the New Age; or, we discover the green pastures and the still waters — at the very heart of the New Age!

The "Still" has been blown! "Be still and know!"

"He maketh me to lie down in Green Pastures; He leadeth me beside the still waters. He restoreth my soul."

This is the saving word for our day!

CHAPTER III
What Do You Mean — He Restoreth My Soul?

"He restoreth my soul."
Psalm 23:3

The valley of the shadow is real; we all pass through it. Some of us live there. Our souls are heavy laden. "He restoreth my soul;" there is hope.

Recently, I heard an Army chaplain who had been stationed overseas speaking on this text. He had read the 23rd Psalm in family devotions. His little girl had brightly come up with the question, "But, Daddy, what do you mean, 'He restoreth my soul'?" Her father answered by reviewing the cases that had come to him for counseling the week before. Here was a mother with two little children whose husband was being shipped out to Viet Nam. What could it mean to her, "He restoreth my soul?" A couple whose home was breaking up in a kind of a hell of hate and bitterness had come to the chaplain. What would it mean to them, "He restoreth my soul?" A young man had come to him completely broken in moral life, his whole lifestyle exploding about him, everything going to pieces. What could this word of hope have meant to him in his moral struggle?

The chaplain, then, answered his little girl: "Honey, you remember when you broke your doll and you were crying like your heart would break, and Mama came and picked you up and held you and hugged you tight and said she would fix the doll, and, then somehow, everything was all right. That's what it means, 'He restoreth my soul.' "

In the terrible death and destruction of an earthquake, what would it mean if people had no faith in God to help them through and beyond the tragedy? What does it mean to adults like us in life situations that are difficult and frightening and confusing? What does it mean to young people who are up against it, trying to find what makes sense in this sort of world? **It means, that when we let him, God picks us up, hugs us a** second, shakes us a bit, if necessary, puts us on our feet, and, if need be, turns us around, straightens us out, opens a door before us and starts us off again, putting new life into us. That is what it means, "He restoreth my soul."

Life is full of tragedy and hurt. That's why we need the restoring powers. One writer reminds us:

> *"One businessman I know gets up in the morning with an anxiety, and jumps anxiously from one anxiety to the next until he goes to bed, and then keeps himself awake with more anxieties."*

Hasn't anybody told him about a God who heals and restores?

Someone else lines up generations of pessimism and hopelessness:

> *"Great grandfather in the Flemish bogs*
>   *Thought the world was going to the dogs.*
> *Grandfather in a house of logs*
>   *Was sure the world was going to the dogs.*
> *Father on an assembly line of cogs*
>   *Declared the world was going to the dogs.*
> *And we in the mists of atom fogs*
>   *Say, also, the world is going to the dogs."*

If we keep saying it, it will go to the dogs. Let's change the word to hope: "He restoreth my soul."

One mother tells me that she wakes up at 6 a.m. and thinks of 12 things she needs to worry about. She spends so much time worrying that she hasn't the time nor the energy left to handle life's normal problems. Handling life's problems creatively is what life is all about. He has restored my soul, again and again.

The soul, the spirit is the most important part of life. I live on a mountain in Asheville, North Carolina. A few years ago, the Secretary of the Navy and his family took off as passengers in a plane from our airport. As it gained altitude it collided with a small plane and 78 lives were lost in the accident. Some people realize the meaning of life rather quickly and move on into its effective fulfillment. Some people are slow starters and mature very slowly in spiritual experience. On that plane there were many who hadn't really started to live; and, yet, in a flash it was all over, ended. Had they been blinded by the footlights of life, and so worried about their costumes and make-up that they had failed to realize the true realities of living?

Some of these people on the plane had gone to church the previous Sunday. I wonder if they realized the power of God to bridge the gap from this life into the next life? I wonder if they understood the ongoing of being, in the fulfillment of personality in a greater wavelength of existence. I wonder if they were aware of heaven, and were ready for it. I wonder if they had grown in soul maturity in that last worship service. I wonder if the preacher that Sunday realized the eternal personal importance of his message. They did not know what would happen; we do not know what will happen. But we do know that in an encounter with a Christ-like God, if we let him into our lives, he can handle any situation in this life or in the next life, "He restoreth my soul."

Some years ago I read a best seller, *Tell No Man,* by Adela Rogers St. John. This novel had keen insight into the moral breakdown of our contemporary way of life. The story was woven around a little group of wealthy people in Chicago. These families were going to pieces. Their lives were breaking down because of constant drinking and because of marital infidelity. They were living by no spiritual structure, no commandments, no ethical disciplines. They were following their own unrestricted desires. Everything they touched, and all that they loved, was beginning to be damned and destroyed by those same undisciplined desires.

In the midst of their undirected living, one of their group, Colin Rowe, jumped from the top of one of the tall buildings of downtown Chicago. The shock of this suicide began to make the group ask questions and dig more deeply into the real meaning of life. They started their quest from their own shallow base: "What was the matter with him? He had everything, didn't he? A wife like Lib; they were going to make him a vice president in June. They had just brought back a Mercedes-Benz from Frankfort. He was shooting in the low 70s. What did he want, for Chrissake?"

In their blindness, this was their question. But they had overlooked some very simple facts: The terror of an agonizing guilt, the burning of a ruptured conscience, the normal hunger of a living soul. In their mad wealth they had forgotten all this. Do we have to play the record over and over again to get the message? Life spells it out for us in blazing letters. When we stop to look and listen we see the inevitable consequences.

Even as far back as the Old Testament, life spelled it out in vivid terms. David committed adultery. It hasn't changed. Ancient times and modern times are the same. The data processing of conscience very quickly feels the burning of moral breakdown. And our sins set up a chain reaction on their own. Uriah, a good soldier, was murdered on the front line. Something in the heart of David was destroyed. The spiritual life of a nation was shaken. A baby was born and lost its life. The sons of David turned out badly, Absalom being caught by his hair in a tree, and killed. Tragedy stalked the house of David. The data processing is inexorable. But the house of David could still be "established in righteousness." So could the house of Colin Rowe, But Colin jumped!

God was heartbroken at David's breakdown, so he moved in on David. He spoke to David through his prophet: "David, see what you have done; look at those you have destroyed." The eyes of David were opened; he saw; he repented; he asked forgiveness; he received forgiveness. His soul was restored.

God would do the same for any of us. But we are blind. The shock of life should open our eyes. But Colin Rowe jumped. He didn't know enough of the love of Christ to realize that he could be forgiven. He didn't have enough faith to realize that Christ could sustain him in a brand new pattern of life. He jumped, and his friends stumbled on. The real controls are not outside, they are inside us. The outside controls cannot keep us or our youth in line, unless we yield to the God-given controls deep inside us (the divine order deep within). By an inner commitment we come into life with real life. "He restoreth my soul by leading me in paths of righteousness — for his name's sake." His name is love! An inner righteousness is always in touch with ultimate reality. And that is the secret of effective living.

Listen to Isaiah:

> "Even youths grow faint and weary,
> . . . but they who wait for the Lord
> shall renew their strength.
> They shall mount up with wings like eagles.
> They shall run and not be weary.
> They shall walk and not be faint."
> (Isaiah 40:30-31)

This can happen to us. I believe in miracles. In a period of tension and strain, I was awakened at 3 a.m. There was a dim light in the room. Suddenly, I felt totally free, completely unburdened, sure, afraid of nothing. I knew a peace that surpassed all understanding. I was renewed, restored. I believe that Christ was in my room that night. "He restoreth my soul." "For me to live, is Christ."

It seems that Colin Rowe's group had lost the secret. Faith wasn't real to them. They believed in miracles yesterday — yes, Christ worked miracles. They believed in miracles tomorrow — yes, some great things are going to happen some day. But they just couldn't accept miracles today. But if there are no miracles today, there are no miracles — ever! So Colin Rowe jumped.

His crowd just didn't believe that one of their own group like Colin Rowe could be drawn into a new evaluation of life, could have a new spirit breathed into him, could again move into an experience of effective living. There was no visible hope

— so he jumped. But this is the kind of gospel that Christ brings into our world. He does restore souls, no matter what the situation. God is just as versatile as that; he moves into the life situation and brings new hope, new fulfillment.

Christianity is a movement of miracles wrought through spiritual power and love. I have seen miracles recently. In fact, they are on the increase. I have seen a hopeless alcoholic become a creative Christian lay man. I have seen a woman healed of a hopeless heart condition. The cardiac surgeon confirmed this. That is why we need a strong, loving Christian fellowship to provide the atmosphere for healing. He restoreth our souls in the midst of life's tensions and many times the soul restores the body.

A high school boy once came to me for counseling. He was in deep trouble. His father had died a year before as an alcoholic. He had no one to turn to. He said he couldn't possibly talk to his mother. Here is the way he put it: "There is a big wall between me and my mother. I can't get over it; I can't get under it; I can't get around it. I've tried and tried, but there is no door in it; there is not a loose brick. If I could only push a brick back and talk to her just a little bit; but I can't get through to her. I've got to talk to somebody — will you listen?"

"Sure I'll listen," was my answer.

He poured his heart out. In this conversation God broke in and helped a high school boy again feel love and forgiveness. Purpose and hope were restored and he could begin to find himself as a real person in the midst of his own world. For youth, this is what it means: "He restoreth my soul."

Many young persons are crying out: "Please mother, please God, please teacher, please world, please government — please understand us; how us the way; give us something to live for and to live by. We have some living to do. We need to be born into real life. There is something unique and infinite in us."

As the adult world, let's get our act together. Let's live it before them. Let's lead them into the real and satisfying dimensions of life. Let's help them find their greatest place of usefulness in today's world. Let's share with them visions and character; integrity and a zest for living. They want it; down deep they want it — they are hungry and scared. Pastors and parents and teachers and business leaders can combine to form the restoring team, active in our contemporary world.

We don't get rid of darkness by shoving it out. We get rid of darkness by letting the light in. But at times we do not want too much light. It shocks us. It unmasks us. It makes us see ourselves as we really are. Then we have to ask ourselves, "How could I have been so stupid?" Perhaps it takes some of this before we can clear the decks and let God restore us into full being. Perhaps some of Colin Rowe's friends found new life because of the shock of his jumping to his death.

Too many of us are spiritual drop-outs: "I've been down so long; down don't worry me no more." We've got money; why do we need God? Colin Rowe had money, but he took his life. We have good minds; we are smart, intelligent; we want to work out our own problems — why do we need God? Yes, we can handle it up to a point; but there is a dimension beyond which I cannot go alone. "The lines on our faces, the ulcers in our stomachs, our trips to the psychiatrist, our high blood pressure all reveal that we are living a second-hand relationship with reality. We act as if we were not aware of a restoring force in the universe. We are not experiencing the face of an all-powerful caring God who is like Jesus. Colin Rowe jumped.

There are some things I just can't handle alone. They are too big for me. Why can't I come down off my high horse and let God help me. "I am the vine, you are the branches," Jesus said. "Without me, you can do nothing." Not really. Beyond the rumblings of evil and death, I hear another sound: the whispers of love and peace. Something is happening in the world that man did not initiate. There is the beginning of an awakening. A Great new day is in the making. God calls you and me to be a part of it. He restoreth my soul for a purpose.

Into the wilderness of this world, Christ comes. Whether it be Chicago or my city, he seeks to save us and to walk with us and to guide us and to strengthen us. He enters our own particular hells in order to deliver us. We know what he stands for. We feel his love and his strength and our belief in ourselves is revived. His forgiveness reaches even my sin and your sin. His love includes us all. "He that cometh to me, I will in no way cast out." His promises are true. He has spoken in my life; he has spoken in yours. Remember the thief on the cross. That thought could have saved Colin Rowe. Too often he has spoken to us and we have walked away. He calls out, "Wait. Don't go away. Don't hang up. I want to talk to you. I want to help you." How many Colin Rowe's have we told, "Christ loves you. Christ wants to help you." Christ enables us to survive even death itself. If Colin Rowe had gotten the message, he could have been a blessing to Chicago. But, "He (Christ) came unto his own, and his own received him not." We can change all that.

Look at the old priest in the story, *The Kappillan of Molta*. The people were forced to live in caves during the terrible bombing that lasted more than a year. There were three or four raids a day. In the midst of all this suffering and terror moved the loving figure of Father Salvatore. The altar of the church was set up in one of the caves. The old priest ministered in love and faith to the living and the dying. He represented the constant presence of Christ. He baptized the babies, he married the young couples, he ministered to the sick, he gave them hope. When it was all over they realized that they were better men, better women, better children because of the suffering and because of a spiritual presence. Their souls had been restored and sustained.

He leads us through the wilderness of life, and gives it meaning. He enables us to face the winds of life, no matter how hard they blow; and when the winds cease their blowing, and our work is done; when our mission is accomplished, and our life fulfilled, then by his grace we shall be ready, whatever the time or the situation, we shall be ready.

That is what it means: "He restoreth my soul."

There is always something more "Beyond the valley of the shadow."

CHAPTER IV
A Straight Path In A Crooked World

"He leadeth me in paths of righteousness for his name's sake."
                    Psalm 23:3

The more confused a society, the more necessary are examples of righteousness. The contrast is that between light and darkness. If we do not let our light shine, the darkness takes over. How terrible to live in a world of total blackness without a spot of light. Christ lighted the lamp; we must keep it shining. If we are on the wrong road, going in the wrong direction, there is little hope. The path of righteousness leads home, to eternal life. That's where the Good Shepherd is leading us.

"He leadeth me in paths of righteousness for his name's sake." The Good Shepherd cannot put up with just any kind of living. He wouldn't be good, if he allowed the sheep to destroy each other. If we have taken poison, we may survive only by the use of a stomach pump. "Come ye out from among them. Be ye separate." We are admonished. Christ delivers us from evil and restores us in righteousness. The misuse of life is Hell.

Into this milieu of lostness, God comes upon a cross. That is the only way he can get the attention of such a world. He suffers with us, and upon our privileged hells he opens the door of hope. He restores my soul by leading me into right living. Back in the days of propeller planes, my wife and I were returning from England, flying all night long across the Atlantic. As always, I was looking out the window. I was watching a bright star just off the tip of the wing. Every 20 minutes the plane would shift to the right and my star would move ahead of us. This bothered me. Was our pilot lost? Then I caught on. He was having to correct our course because we were being blown off course by a strong north wind. The pilot was compensating for the wind drift.

When was the last time we checked our course? Where are we going to end up if we keep this course? Are we really growing as Christians, or are we gradually giving in to the pagan lifestyle of the world about us? Are we on course toward the city of God, or are we drifting? We check our course by our understanding of God and what he wants for us. We check by the spirit and life that we see in Jesus. That night I didn't correct our course; the pilot did. I cannot maintain my life course, alone. God guides me and enables me, when I let him.

The Psalmist reaches out for the effective concern of God for our lives:

> *Have mercy on me, O God, according to thy loving kindness: according unto the multitude of thy tender mercies blot out my transgressions.*
>
> *Wash me thoroughly from my iniquity, and cleanse me from my sin . . . .*
>
> *Behold thou desireth truth in the inward parts: and in the hidden part thou shalt make me to know wisdom . . . .*
>
> *Create in me a clean heart, O God, and renew a right spirit within me . . . .*
>
> *Restore unto me the joy of thy salvation; and uphold me with thy free spirit.*
>
> (Psalm 51:1-12 — Selected verses)

Again and again I have felt my life's course corrected by an invisible, but wise and loving hand.

They say that "dishonest mortar" was responsible for the terrible destruction of the San Francisco earthquake. This might also account for the terrible death toll of other earthquakes. Sadly we admit that there is much "dishonest mortar" in us, in our nation, in our world today. Our civilization may be about to collapse about us. But God does not want it to. Our Bible is the textbook for moral and ethical living. But it is evident that we are not living by the text. It frightens us, these overpowering forces of evil active in the world about us. I fear that we are not only the victims of evil but also, sadly, a part of the cause.

I was intrigued by an article written by David Chaney. He suggested that it would be nice if we all lived in "Gotham" where all the evil was visible, separate, outside ourselves. It would be great to have "Batman and Robin" destroy all this evil, and let us go on undisturbed about our business and pleasure. But life is not set up that way. The battle between good and evil is not outside us, but inside us.

The face of evil is nine-tenths hidden. Evil is the original fifth column. Its infiltration is subtle and deep. No Batman can save us; for we, the people, are the villain. Evil is not separate from man; it is deep in man's nature. The battle between good and evil is not fought out in the air over the rooftops of Gotham. It is constantly being fought out in the souls of men, where selfishness, greed, blindness, lust, prejudice and littleness corrupt the heart and destroy human relationships.

The novel, *The Hall of Mirrors*, by John Wilson, shocked me awake, as I looked at myself and my fellow human beings in the "hall of mirrors." Sir Thomas Gilling, the most respected medical person in all of England, was involved in a lawsuit with Dr. Lines. As the trial proceeded, we discovered that in the courtroom even a great man's rationalizations will not stand up before cross examination. Under legal bombardment, Sir Thomas, himself, begins to see how from a depressing childhood he had allowed his ambitions to break the heart of his father, to make him lose the girl that he loved, to push him into a life on the surface great, powerful and respected, but in the light of inner truth, eaten out, full of holes and ambiguities. At the end of the trial, he sadly remarks: "Perhaps all men of his age and station should be stripped naked before the world, for the good of their souls." Then he adds, "It was not everyone who was privileged with a dress rehearsal of judgment day." Through some experience like this we might all find how far we have missed the straight path.

In this trial we see life revealed. Mistakes can be made. And often we claim more for a situation than there is in it. Sir Thomas Gilling observed: "I had known this in my heart since childhood." God gives to us the gift of appraising ourselves in depth, so that we really know when our integrity is valid, and when we are playing false. These awful things revealed in the courtroom happened to normal people living normal lives. They were destroyed by facts. These things can happen to some people like you and me, when we allow emotions and motives, pressures, prejudices and half-truths to get all mixed up in our relationships with other people.

At times the face of evil is hidden deep within one's own subconscious nature. "Cleanse thou me from secret faults," O God. These things haunt us. Some people go to the psychiatrist in order to get these hidden ambiguities dug out of the depths of their subconscious. Christ has a way with hidden evil. When a person can honestly seek his love, his strength, his wholeness, and accept this deep in their subconscious being; then Christ invades the subconscious, and in his own presence drives out the evil, puts love and right in its place, heals the wound and releases a new person into life.

A terrifying sequence in Michael Crichton's book, *Sphere*, illustrates this. Trained in engineering, Norman, Harry and Beth descend 1,000 feet to the ocean floor in a kind of depth laboratory to investigate a strange space ship discovered there. In the process many dangers were encountered, and Beth and Harry were so disoriented that they tried to kill Norman. He escaped and activated a small transit submarine to reach the surface, 1,000 feet above. He had only 19 minutes before a terrific explosion would crush the lab and the submarine. Nineteen minutes before death.

Norman had decided that it was right to leave them to die to save his own life. As the tiny vessel rose rapidly toward the surface, a battle was waged between good and evil deep within his soul. "I am justified; they tried to kill me." The minutes were flying by. Beth's voice came over the intercom, "Save me! Save me!" Norman's response was that it was too late.

He couldn't save them and save himself. He was right, he was sure. As he was about to reach the surface and safety with 14 minutes before the explosion, that deeper consciousness would not let him go on. His surface mind was saying: "I hate them. It's not my responsibility. I want to save myself." But he had to go back, even though he was afraid to go back. He was right at the surface, and was free. "I must go back; but if I go back I will die."

"He pressed the controls halting his ascent. As he started back down, he saw that his hands were shaking." They were 1,000 feet below and there were only 14 minutes left before death.

It was awful. He got to the bottom. He had to break into the depth lab. The hatches were all locked. He finally got in. The warning system kept calling the time, 10 and then 9 minutes till the explosion. Harry was unconscious; Beth was crazy. He had to get them into their diving suits, with the minutes ticking away. He got them out and into the transit submarine against impossible odds.

He started their ascent. "Attention please," the computer called out, "one minute 20 seconds till explosion." It would take 2½ minutes to get to the surface. They could be crushed by the explosion. They reached the 800-foot depth and Harry cried out, "We'll never make it." "Thirty seconds." "Ten seconds," Harry continued, "Nine . . . eight. Brace yourself." The explosion rocked them, turned them upside down, then sent them up in a giant surge. They burst out on the surface. Harry was screaming, "We did it! We did it!" They were alive.

Norman mused, psychologist that he was, "as consciousness widened, there was still more unconsciousness beyond. There was always more, just beyond reach." In his struggle, Norman had broken beyond selfish consciousness into the infinite consciousness of the Eternal. And that was where the ultimate right was. He had tapped it; or it had tapped him. The deep inner truth had overcome his surface rationalizations, and he was saved. "He leadeth me in the paths of righteousness for his name's sake." He does, he does, if we let him.

But we must listen to that deep inner whisper that denies our rationalizations.

In a terrible air plane explosion in England a number of years ago, human bodies were scattered over 15 miles; where was God in all of this? The hidden face of God is just as much a problem as the hidden face of evil. What is God doing? God is right in the middle of this, with the living and with the dying, seeking in the struggles of life and death to bring his struggling children through to mature spiritual life, ready for the Eternal. God is in the suffering of Christ revealing his true self to a suffering humanity. God is in the struggle for justice in a world not yet perfected. A Batman Messiah will not swoop in and do it all for us, while we sleep or pursue our pleasures, uninvolved. The Christ in us seeks to defeat the evil in us, and thus saves us and saves the world.

Does he lead us in paths of righteousness? God is in Christ, invading his world with love sufficient eventually to defeat the world's evil. God is incarnate in the midst of life's crises and conflicts. Christ still suffers on the cross that continues to be built by man's evil, and in his suffering breaks the back of that evil, and slowly is bringing humanity to sanity and to love. God is continually in Christ breaking the power of the crucifixion by the power of the resurrection. In the process of life, the hidden face of God is revealed in the final victory of love, and through the struggles of our own sweat and blood and tears.

This is the secret: "Christ in you," the hope of victory over the evil of the world. The hope of the new age. Christ in you wrestling with drugs, with home problems, with youth problems, with corporate problems, with world problems — working constantly at the problems of our world. This is the moving power changing and transforming us. Christ in you, saving the world. No evil can stand against Christ alive in humanity. Christ made alive in us, this is our potential — "The Grace of God that taketh away the sins of the world." He promises to lead us in "paths of righteousness."

With all this in mind we dare to look at America at this moment of history. At some time in the future, historians may look back and say: "America fell out of her own excesses." They were a great nation of ideals zapped into oblivion by permissive immorality. They forgot the basic values that must be transmitted to children as the source of their future strength and vitality. Before her fall, a large percent of her population indulged, in an orgy of self-pampering, overdosing, loafing, sponging, splurging, cheating, playing fast and loose with corporate money, shoplifting, looting, philandering, disregard of marital ties and parental responsibilities, and even murder. There were child prostitutes, spouse-swapping, youth addicted to sex-exciting movies and television scenes, millions of alcoholics, drug addicts everywhere, vice displayed openly on the streets and no remorse shown. They were no longer willing to work. They were content with sub-standard workmanship until other nations took over the world market. They were content to live on borrowed money and had not the character to face it and begin paying back their mounting deficit. Their members of congress were taking bribes and putting friends on the public payroll. Their schools and universities had abandoned the responsibility for the moral development of their students. The military industrial complex was bleeding their economy to death. Sex was for sale everywhere; it was a part of business promotion. Their media was glorifying all of this and promoting it.

The historians may say, "For 300 years America was a miracle to all the world . . . but they squandered their heritage. It's a wonder they survived as long as they did."

As we look at ourselves in the Hall of Mirrors, we are not surprised to see this description of New York written by Bryon Rufus Newton and copied in *The Saturday Review:*

> *Vulgar of manner, overfed,*
> *overdressed and underbred:*
> *Heartless, Godless, Hell's delight;*
> *Rude by day and lewd by night;*

> *Bedwarfed the man, o'ergrown the brute,*
> *Ruled by ($) and prostitute;*
> *Purple-robed and pauper-clad,*
> *Raving, rotting, money-mad;*
> *A squirming herd in mammon's mesh,*
> *A wilderness of human flesh;*
> *Crazed with avarice, lust and rum,*
> *New York, thy name's delirium.*

The little Christian church in Corinth found itself crushed by a similar pagan environment. Paul, writing to them with the insight of the Holy Spirit, warned them: "I could not speak to you as spiritual, but as physical, even as unto babes in Christ (1 Corinthians 3:1)." Perhaps we in the church today are just physical, not spiritual. We do not speak and act as spiritually empowered persons; we are just stumbling physical persons. A Christian is to be given spiritual awareness, spiritual power. As spiritual persons we can be sustained in righteousness and be an example and an encouragement to the community around us. Only then are we "light" and "yeast" for the saving of the world in our time. And now we become effective agents of love and righteousness in the life of a dying world. Paul encourages us: "We are laborers together with God: you are God's handiwork, you are God's building (1 Corinthians 3:9)." The spiritual is the ultimate truth; the physical, alone, just won't cut it.

Before it's too late, could we repent and cry out, "out of the depths have we cried unto thee, O God." There is still a chance. History has not closed the door, yet. All through the scriptures there is the promise: "I will lead you out of captivity." "I will save you." "I will restore you in righteousness." "I will yet lead you in paths of righteousness for my name's sake," sayeth our God.

It has been quaintly said: "Satan might come into your back yard. But you don't have to put an umbrella over him; fan him, feed him and serve him ice cold lemonade." Too many of us are giving in, little by little until we are supporting evil.

But the power that lifts us up is greater than the power that drags us down. There are still millions of good people in America. There is a strong remnant. And God brought that remnant back to Jerusalem again and again.

But that was when they repented, prayed and followed.

Paul directs us: "Don't let the world squeeze you into its mold; but let God remold your mind from within (Romans 12:2)." Be in the world, but be not of the world. Christians should live in the world, be a part of it, but not be dominated by it. Christians are not to be narrow, stiff, self righteous; but loving, healing, helping. They are to show moral stamina, character, humility, winsomeness. They are to change the world by serving the world." For God has called us out of darkness into his marvelous light." I cannot change America; but I can let God change me; and that will help change America.

Many families are now at the crossroads; which way will it be? Will we take the shortcuts, or the real highway to the city of God? We belong either to the evil forces at work in our country, or we belong to Christ.

Let us do our own thinking. Don't yield to unchristian standards. Don't let the boss or business pressures force us to give in to unchristian practices. We can become a part of an oasis of love and high moral living in the midst of a confused, mixed-up world. We can help arrest the avalanche of national moral let-down and decay. I will say "no" to the wrong and "yes" to the right. By the grace of God we can have the courage to belong to Christ. This is made possible by a Christ-possessed mind.

We worship God not only at church, but in the home, at work, and in all life's relations. It takes a genuine break with evil and a true devotion to the good. We will never get beyond the valley of the shadows except by the paths of righteousness.

"He leadeth me in paths of righteousness for his name's sake."

CHAPTER V
Finding God In The Narrows Of Life

"Yea though I walk through the valley of the shadow of death, I will fear no evil: for thou art with me; thy rod and thy staff they comfort me."
                              Psalm 23:4

There is a little book, *My Shepherd Life in Galilee*, written by Habauch. He had been a shepherd in Galilee and could write with understanding. Listen, as he describes an incident. It was late in the evening, when the shadows were already creeping across the barren land of Palestine. He was leading his sheep toward the fold. As the darkness descended, he had to lead his flock through a very narrow ravine. Very little light could penetrate to the bottom of the gorge. He was seeking a small open place beyond the ravine, where the sheepfold was. He could feel the fear of the sheep, threatened by the dangers of the narrow ravine. As they were crowded by the ravine the sheep pressed upon the shepherd. In pressing against him they found comfort, warmth and strength. But that was not all. As the shepherd was crowded by the sheep, as they pressed against him, he experienced a warmth, a glow of satisfaction and a joy, because the sheep needed him and found strength in him. Both the shepherd and the sheep found each other in the dark narrows of the canyon. And the shepherd was pleased.

Now we get the complete picture of the give and take of faith. Perhaps it is in the crises of life, as you and I have to face them, in the narrows of life where we are crowded in against God, that we begin to know him and find strength and hope, faith and joy. We see beneath the shallow surface of life and begin to experience peace. And, surprisingly, we begin to glimpse an even deeper fact, that while I am being crowded in on God, that God is experiencing joy because his children are beginning to discover him again and draw close to him and glimpse eternal things. Perhaps it is most in the valley of the shadow that we face reality, and grow in the joy of divine fellowship.

But there are still problems. Not everyone enters the valley of the shadow with faith. Some enter only with bitterness, and this is utter lostness. Some are so hardened that they cry out, "There is no God." Some are so crushed that they ask: "Why has God done this to me?" Others cry out: "I can't take it," and then collapse. They would not admit that the Shepherd was there. God even understands these, and loves them; he seeks to enter into their bewilderment and lead them through the valley into a broad and open life of faith. God does not get mad at us in our struggles; he draws closest to those who are having the hardest time. The narrows are not a dead-end street. Stay with it in trust and you will discover that the valley of the shadow opens up in God's presence and at the gates of the eternal. Life is going somewhere; but ravines are a part of the journey. The path through to the other side of the shadow is discovered through the passport of faith.

In the valley of the shadow there is light. "Thou art with me." The splendor of God breaks through. Here we are forced into an awareness of God, or we do not survive.

There is a plaintive story by Christine Anthony that came out of the last war: *I Am Fifteen And I Don't Want To Die.* I am much more than 15 and I don't want to die — not yet. Life is meaningful and I want to hold on to it. God made us that way. The picture back of the story is that of a very dark valley. A family is trapped in a flooded basement in the siege of Budapest. Close your eyes and see it: The water is rising, the basement is crowded with refugees; it's dark, there is no food, little hope; there is death on the outside in the street, there is death on the inside. This is the valley of the shadow. At first, the darkness is all that we can see; then, strangely, a kind of light glows in the darkness. You can't tell where it is coming from. Now we begin to understand. In the midst of all this fear, you begin to realize a courage that matches the fear. In the midst of hate, there appears a love that outweighs the hate. Here in a situation created by greed, hate and injustice, you begin to see in this little group of people a self-forgetfulness and a self-giving that is greater than the prevailing threat.

There was Pista, a Hungarian soldier, separated from his command; though a stranger, he joined himself to this tiny despairing group huddled in the basement. We see him going out every day into the streets of death, risking capture or death. One day he went to find sulfa drugs for an old man who had pneumonia and was facing death in the damp cold basement. Somehow he found a little apothecary shop in one of the tiny alleys of the doomed city. The next day he goes for canned milk for a starving baby whose mother could not feed him. The next it's candles for the darkness. The next day Pista goes after a priest because the old man is dying and needs confession. Pista stays out there under fire until he finds a priest and brings him to the basement, where the priest also marries Eve and Gabriel who love each other and want to marry before they die. Pista moves in and out of the scene as an angel of mercy. And you see God in Pista — the mystery of God who can produce such a boy in this young soldier who gave his life to help others.

More than this, you see God in the love of the little mother for her baby; you see God in the love of Eve for Gabriel; you see God in the courageous love of the old priest who came and ministered to them with the gentleness of Christ. You see God in people, there in the valley of the shadow; and you see God there in the spirit working night and day on his own. God in the shadows, God in the narrows, holding his children close to him. This little group never forgot the strange spiritual presence that was so real in those hopeless days. God in the narrows, pressing in upon the people; they pressing upon him and pressing in on each other until they became a community.

In that basement they were facing death. They could have fought each other for every crust of bread. But something happened in that darkness. They felt each other's pain; they undergirded each other's weakness; they shared each other's suffering and each other's joy. This is what God wants in his world. Maybe this is the meaning of the cross. God allows crisis in life so that falseness may be burned away and his children discover the deep and beautiful meaning of love.

Traveling in England soon after the last war I experienced two meaningful surprises. Some English friends were showing us around Plymouth. We were viewing the ruins of Plymouth, the devastated buildings, the places where buildings had been and were no more. Our friends had lived through the saturation bombing of Plymouth. They described the terror of death every night, the fire bombs, the falling buildings, and they underneath the whole business. Friends were being killed, loved ones were losing their lives. Then a strange thing happened: they revealed to us a kind of nostalgia. They were saying: "Well, there was such a sense of oneness then. People cared so much for each other; they were really concerned for all their neighbors. They did everything they possibly could for each other. People suffered with each other. There was a wonderful spirit of oneness in those days." It is strange how God really brings people together in the narrows of life.

Later I took a taxi from Stratford on Avon down to Birmingham late at night. Before we had driven far, the driver began talking about the war. He said: "My father was a firefighter. I was a little boy. Every night my father had to go out and fight the flames, as fire bombs continued to rain down. I never knew whether my father would come home alive. We lived this way, day after day." Then he added, "You know, everybody was somebody in those days; everybody believed in each other. Everybody supported everybody else." As my taxi driver was describing all this, it actually seemed that he was homesick for the old spirit of caring, of everybody being somebody. This sounds strange; but somehow in the valley of the shadow the realities of life come to the surface, the presence of God is vividly near. At times God leads his children through the narrows so they discover real life again and rise above their selfish blindness.

I have seen *The Lost Colony* twice; it plays on Roanoke Island off the coast of North Carolina. We looked at this little group of men and women and one baby crowded into their small wooden fortress. They were in a foreign land, surrounded by hostile Indians. England had forgotten them, because of the war with Spain. Some of them were being killed every day. It was a picture of despair.

But something else appears: Their faith, their love, how they stood together. You remember their stubborn dream of a new world about to be born. They suffered and disappeared, but the dream lived. Under God the dream lived and we are here today. The dream came out of the valley of the shadow, out of the narrows of life.

I remembered Old Tom, the drunken bum, who was probably "shanghaied." He probably got drunk in England and awoke on Roanoke Island. But Tom found himself, came to himself, in the struggles of their dangerous plight. We see Tom, alone, standing guard on the wall of the fortress while all the others, exhausted, slept around the tiny fire within the palisade. The old drunk, the no-good, up there standing guard, alone. He is heard to whisper: "Tom, the wilderness hath made a man of thee." And that was the truth, he had become a man. He had found himself, he had come to himself, in the wilderness, in the valley of the shadow.

This was the secret power of the early Christians. Hiding out in the catacombs under Rome, being killed every day. They had seen Stephen stoned to death. But God was so visible in their plight. The Christ was with them; they carried on until the church was born. They sang the Psalms of hope; they quoted and quoted again this Psalm 23. The blaze of the kingdom of Christ was visible to them; and they made the dream visible to others. They were forced in upon God; and God was glad to be in their midst. They stood as one person against the terrors of their day.

The apostle Paul lived in the valley of the shadow and he knew that for him to live was Christ, or he wouldn't make it. It was out of the narrows and crises of life that Paul cried out: "In shipwreck, in beatings, in prison, in death, in all these things; in tribulation, in distress, in persecution, in famine, in peril and sword; not separate from these things, not apart from these things; but walking right through the perils of life." That's where God is incarnate. Christ, God is in Christ, in the midst of life — real life — the life we live every day. This is the victory: God in the midst of life — Christ with us — coming into the existence, into our crises to bring us through into life's eternal fulfillment.

When a person comes face to face with death and survives, there is something indelible etched on his memory. I have faced it, and I know others who have faced it. It is like a flash of lightning on a dark night. The blazing images linger in your mind after the light is gone. Years later, you still see what you saw in the flash of lightning. The crises of life, the valley of shadows, bring reality to the soul; they reveal God to man. Somehow the meaning of life is seen vividly.

Several years ago my wife and I were in an automobile accident. By the grace of God we came through without being hurt. But we vividly remember every detail, every second, every move of the car, our own feelings and our thoughts at that moment. All this written on our minds and souls, forever. You face death and reality comes clear; only a deep sigh of gratitude to God is the inescapable answer. You are still alive; the sun still shines. You are still with your loved ones, you can still carry on in the midst of life — the glory of it all — God realized in a moment of possible tragedy. This photographic exposure leaves you a bigger better person. You become of age.

Douglas Steere reminds us that we all die many little deaths and that we learn from these little deaths. I remember my mother's death when I was a boy: The separation was a shock; the loss was deep. And, yet, I emerged from this little death a new person, with a realization of new responsibilities, and with a new sense of the full dimensions of life that depended on me now as a person. Later when my father died I went through a little death of lostness, separation, but also new birth, a new facing up to life as a man now totally on my own.

Once, as a small boy, I got very sick as we were visiting in the country about seven miles from a doctor. I was scared; I thought I was going to die, but I didn't. Through this little death I became a bigger boy, a wiser boy; I was beginning to be a man. It all happened in the valley of the shadow.

In many ways, at this moment, America is going through the valley. We see the concentration of evil; we admit our lack of commitment, our lack faith. We are frightened, and ought to be. God is saying something to us in the narrows. He is demanding that we discover values, that we come to a new dedication to truth and integrity, that we accept the truth of love and affection, that we accept a new sense of destiny based on moral values and righteousness. Again and again the love of God shocks us into a new awareness.

Rufus Jones, a great practical mystic, writes about an experience in his own life. He was despondent over the loss of his son. In his despondency he was walking aimlessly down the street of a great city. All of a sudden he noticed a tiny girl run down those brownstone steps. She ran through a great iron gate out onto the sidewalk. The gate slammed shut behind her and it locked itself. When the little girl realized what she had done —that she had shut herself out of her familiar world, her home, her loved ones — she rushed back to the gate. She held on to the iron bars; she shook it and beat upon it. She screamed and waited, but she couldn't get in. She was trapped in a strange, hostile world. All of a sudden the door to the great house swung open. The mother rushed down the steps, opened the gate, picked up the child in her arms and said: "Honey, didn't you know I'd come? Didn't you know I would come?" In his personal despair, Rufus Jones walked on down the street, but he says: "Now I knew that there was love behind my own shut gate." God had led him through the valley and back into faith, and there was peace. He now knew in his own broken heart that God would take care of his son in his death, and that God would take care of him in his sorrow.

The story of the thief on the cross next to Christ has always intrigued me. I am grateful that the New Testament recorded that incident. It opens the door of hope. A thief, a bad man who had misused his life, is being executed on the cross next to Jesus. In the agony of crucifixion, the dying thief saw the emptiness, the uselessness, the evil of his own life. He saw the real meaning of life revealed in the gentle, loving, forgiving person dying on the cross next to him. (And Christ is always on the cross next to ours — don't forget it.) The thief couldn't understand it; but he saw that love was real. God broke into his mind and revealed himself to the dying man. All heaven broke loose. The thief cried out with his last breath: "Master, Master, remember me when you come into your kingdom." He was beholding the open-endedness of life. It was not a dead-end street. Life was going somewhere and he wanted to go. Jesus, in spite of his own agony turned his head and whispered: "This day shall thou be with me in Paradise." A wandering child of God had been snatched out of the narrows of life into the vast, loving openness of the eternal. It took God two crosses to bring about that miracle: The thief's cross of revelation and need; Jesus' cross of love and forgiveness. If all this is open to a repenting thief, surely it is open to you and me: God has a next step in every crisis, for us personally, or for our nation or for our world. But we have to accept it.

Christ on a cross, Christ in the narrows, Christ beyond the narrows; Christ in the resurrection. It is in this mystery that I rediscover hope, and by this hope we are saved. And in this strength we move as the redeemed people of God out into the world to proclaim God's destiny for humanity.

> *Oh, King, oh, Captain, wasted,*
> *Wan with scourging,*
> *Strong beyond our speech*
> *And wonderful with woe.*
> > *Whither, relentlessly,*
> *Wilt thou still be urging*
> *The maimed and halt*
> *That have no strength to go.*
> > *Peace! Peace!*
> *Why must we love thee so?*
> *Because, because He is our hope!*

We do not bring God into the situation, into the narrows of life; God is already there, ministering to his people. We meet him there. We obey and enable God to realize his purposes through us. If need be he wipes away all tears from our eyes — there shall be no more sorrow there. "And there shall be no more death, neither sorrow, nor crying (Revelation 21:4)." We are eternally in the hands of a Christ-like God — a heavenly Father.

And this is the lesson of the valley of the shadow of death: We walk through the valley sustained by an almighty Father who is love. The frightened sheep crowd close to the Shepherd; and God is pleased that his children have come home. We have met him in existence where we struggle; he has led us through to life.

Yea, though I walk
Through the valley of the shadow of death,
I will fear no evil,
For thou are with me.
Thy rod and thy staff
They comfort me —

And fashion a new world!

Thy rod protects us from evil. Thy staff guides us in paths of righteousness. Until we, at last, are home.

CHAPTER VI
Sustained In Time Of Difficulty

"Thou preparest a table before me in the presence of mine enemies...."
Psalm 23:5

How can the past speak to the present? How can the ancient make itself known in the contemporary? Many feel that it cannot — that nothing can be learned from the past — that everything to be learned is in the present and in the future. Perhaps this is where we have missed the true meaning of life.

The segment of the 23rd Psalm we gaze upon in this chapter is: "He prepareth a table before me in the presence of mine enemies." Does it fit anything today? Should we spend time on it? Is there a truth here we have by-passed in the hurried business of life? Does God sustain us as we face the grim challenges of life? Does a table in the presence of our enemies say anything to us?

Recently a medical friend of mine pointed his finger at me and said: "You preachers ought to build up the faith level of your people, so that we doctors would not have to build up the barbiturate level." There is truth here. We have been overlooking the deep reservoirs of life. We have not realized the spiritual powers available to us. We do not lean on God's arm; nor do we fully accept the supporting love of Jesus. So we break down and we burn out. There is an inner support far beyond scientific knowledge. God does prepare a table before us in the presence of our needs. The sustaining love of God is available to us as we face life's crises.

Life is situation living; it is one episode after another. I continually find myself in situation after situation at home, at work, in the neighborhood, in the world. This is where

God meets us — In the wise handling of immediate situations. He sustains us in the face of the demands of life, where the decisions have to be made, when the burdens have to be carried, where the battles have to be fought — where the sweat and the toil and the wrong is. This is where God enters life, preparing a table of sustenance in the presence of the demands of life.

The picture is a desert scene. According to the code of the desert if there is a refugee, someone fleeing for his life, you may receive this individual into your tent and give him sanctuary, protection. A man fleeing for his life. Perhaps he has killed someone by accident. And the dead man's family is pursuing him to take his life. "An eye for an eye, and a tooth for a tooth," still stands in the desert. The man is fleeing, exhausted. They are about to overtake him. He sees them topping out on the last sand dune behind him as he starts down the far side of this dune. And then, all of a sudden, he sees in the little valley below him an encampment of Bedouins. He stumbles down the sand dune and falls on his face in front of the tent of the sheik. The sheik can pay him no mind and leave him there to be murdered. But this sheik takes him in, and he is now under the protection of the sheik. His safety is guaranteed. The sheik will probably prepare a meal in the little canopy of the tent where the refugee can sit and be refreshed, while his enemies have to stay out there on the other side of the line and look on. They can't come in; he is protected.

"He prepareth a table before me in the presence of mine enemies," does make sense. It is the difference between life and death. Here the refugee finds strength and hope. The host might even give him a guard that night after dark and help him sneak away from his pursuers to permanent safety. We are not in the desert; but we stumble into all kinds of needy situations; and we need support in time of crisis. I have caught myself running now and then; and so have you — refugees in the midst of life. Thousands of things pursue us, attack us in this computer, concrete jungle in which we live. Fearful strains and stresses attack us. God invades the crisis to give us strength.

We long for that uplifting, infilling power of hope and assurance where we can catch our breath, realign ourselves, and step once more into life, free from defeat and despair. God does not prepare a tremendous, luscious banquet and sit us down to overeat. He lovingly sustains us. Perhaps he just prepares for us little snacks of sustenance from battle station to battle station along the road to life.

All the time we are fighting battles, making decisions, solving problems, overcoming difficulties. It's rough out here in the middle of life. It's finding meaning, getting your teeth into it, producing accomplishments, doing some good for humanity, finding your purpose in the fabric and structure of life. This is where God prepares his table to sustain us.

But sometimes we fail to trust him. We are fleeing in the desert, and just don't believe that God's tent has anything to offer. We stumble by on our own, alone; and flee on deeper and deeper into the desert. We are overtaken and destroyed. We could have turned in, we could have opened up to God in our extremity. We could have done this just to see if God could make a difference, if he could sustain us. We would have discovered reservoirs of life to answer our deepest needs. But we didn't risk faith; we risked death instead. Maybe we didn't want God to take hold of our lives. Perhaps we didn't want him to recreate and reconstruct us. Maybe we were afraid to change. We wanted things just as they were. But we had no strength, and we collapsed.

We were fed up with this stupid life, this stupid job, this stupid struggle to get started every morning, and that stupid struggle at home every night, this stupid world, and my stupid self I've got to live with. How did we get caught in this whirlpool of stupidity? How can we escape from it? We try all kinds of stupid ways to escape.

It's amazing! God loved this stupid world so much that he sent Christ to reveal truth and love, to refashion humanity into right relationships, to bring deep satisfaction into the heart of individual persons. You know Christ said a strange thing, though he had been beaten down and crucified by the world.

He said: "Father, don't take these followers of mine out of this stupid world. Father, don't take them out of the world. I gave my life for this world. Keep them in this world, that their spirits touched by thy spirit may bring life to this world. That they may push back the stupidity, bring back meaning and value, and put a shout of joy in the heart of man. That they may open to others the reservoirs of the eternal. That the Jesus Spirit may possess the life of the world. That justice and love may be real in the marketplace and in the halls of government." God, preparing tables before us in the presence of life's demands!

Bishop Welsh lived to be 105 years of age. He deserved a prize just for living that long. But at 104, he was still thinking, writing and speaking. Just before he died he wrote an article for *Reader's Digest*. Here is what he said: "We look at the world, you and I. We want fast progress. And we pray, 'How long, O Lord; How long, how long, O Lord? I can't put up with it. Send us a miracle, O God. Give us peace, O God, this minute.' "

That's the way we feel. I want peace and a cessation of terrorism this minute. That's my impatience. I want it right now; I want it yesterday. But the old Bishop, out of the wisdom of a hundred years, says: "But God answers by littles. God answers by littles." Just a little here, and a little there. A step here and a step there; an inch here and an inch there. But God is moving with deliberate speed, like the hands of a clock. The bishop continued: "In life's situations, when we wanted a miracle to redeem this minute, God sends a baby to redeem the world."

But the Luthers, the Wesleys are awfully far apart; in spite of this, God moves, and he surprises us. He doesn't turn loose. He moves inch by inch, mile by mile, century by century, toward his goals. He doesn't turn loose. He works by littles through us. So that in a strange way it is we who will redeem this world. Redeem it through the eternal trust of God. If our city is to be redeemed, if it is to find goodness and greatness, it will be redeemed by the people of our city, by the churches of our city, by those of us who by faith and open hearts are seeking new meanings and are willing to be different. And all the while God supplies a bountiful buffet of spiritual food to fuel us on our way.

This is how the world will find redemption, not in a minute, but in the slow building of character and vision, in opening the doors of understanding until people no longer want to hate and kill, but build each other up in our march toward the kingdom of God. "He prepares a table before us in the presence of our enemies."

Perhaps this is the picture as we flee from refugee tent to refugee tent in our struggle through life; as we find God's table prepared again and again in our times of extremity, we discover the reality of God's saving presence. It is then that we begin to set up tents in the desert for others in extremity; and point other fleeing refugees from life to the places of refuge and the sustaining tables of our God.

But too many of us are caught, trapped, in the prevailing unfaith of today. The climate of today is atheism, agnosticism, greed. Most of the fiction today follows this trend. It is tragic that when the best brains of our world could be sweating it out seeking new and great avenues of truth, they are wasting their time and our time going round and round on a merry-go-round of doubt, vulgarity and nothingness. So we read our literature based on unfaith and pessimism and discover that subconsciously we are alone in a meaningless, empty universe, going nowhere. We have chosen to feed at the table of hopeless secularism, while before us God has prepared a table of life and purpose. There are other things to read.

David Reed suggests that the word "hopeless" is a blasphemous word. For when we use that word about any situation or person, with a flat finality that slams the door, we deny the God of hope. While hope is alive we feed at the table God has prepared for us and our hope is strengthened. "Faith," Roy Smith reminds us, "never closes our eyes to the difficulties; it opens our eyes to our resources."

If my son will not come to my table, I cannot feed him. And so with God. If God cuts us off — that's cruel (but he doesn't). We are the ones who cut God off — and that is stupid. All the while Isaiah points out the truth of Christ back of the life scene:

> *"Surely he hath borne our griefs,*
> *And carried our sorrows: . . .*
> *He was wounded for our transgressions,*
> *He was bruised for our iniquities:*
> *Upon him was the chastisement that makes us whole;*
> *And with his stripes we are healed."*
>
> Isaiah 53:4-5

A member of my congregation came to me and said, "I don't believe in God. I don't believe in Christ as revealing the Spirit of God in the midst of this world. I just don't believe." How did he get that way? By reading materials with an unbelieving bias. He had not been reading the scriptures, where God comes alive, where Christ walks the paths of this earth. He had turned his back on the table prepared for him. He hadn't come to church; he hadn't mixed with people who were living a life of faith. He was intellectual but at a shallow level; he was brilliant but not wise. He lived in a God-prepared world of plenty, but he was starving to death. He was just going around in circles; he was treading water, barely keeping his head above water.

What had happened to him? Every plant that grows has a frost point. One plant will freeze at 33 degrees, another at 29 degrees, another at 25 degrees. I have snapdragons that have survived the entire winter, and the temperature has been as low as eight degrees. This confused man had dropped below his frost point in his living and reading and thinking. He had frozen. He had died spiritually; he had forgotten to feed his soul. He was brainwashed, but not cleansed.

Out of today's agnosticism we hear strange statements. Recently, someone said to me, referring to the Holy Spirit, "It's just a term to cover up our ignorance." Where did he get that? Is it not true that the Holy Spirit is the living God in the midst of a computer age (or any other age). The spirit of the living God — not covering up ignorance, but exposing ignorance. He is revealing to our brilliant, mixed up minds the simplicities of truth, love and righteousness. Nothing else answers our persistent gnawing questions. How stupid can we get? We pass by the deep clear reservoirs of truth, and drink surface water that is polluted and has no life in it. Christ has set a table of life for us in the midst of the struggles of the present moment.

Many of us have lost God; he is just not real anymore. We lost him in different ways. With some it was a moral problem, with some an intellectual problem. The big problem is that today many persons are living by their doubts. They are proud of their doubt; they worship their unbelief; they are ashamed of faith. Now doubt has its place. Doubt keeps us from being gullible; doubt sharpens the concepts of truth by eliminating the false concepts. Doubt helps us to see the phony, so that we can concentrate on reality. We live by truth; we die by truth. The structure of the universe is truth. God helps us to recognize the truth. To live by doubt is the ultimate despair.

We have doubts; but — we don't live by them. We have doubts; but we live by our faith — what we believe in. We may not have much faith; but we live by what we really believe in, no matter how small. This is what you risk your life on; this is what you give your life to. All of us have a little bit of faith. When we dare to live by it, make our decisions on this basis, then our faith grows and our vision of reality expands. And finally we realize we have come face to face with God.

A few years ago, I sat with a hundred theologians from all over the world. The seminar was held at Oxford University. We were trying to sweat out the realities of basic Christian faith. One evening we listened to Dr. Francis Ayers, head of the Department of Philosophy at Cambridge. He was perhaps the world's leading atheist. He spoke brilliantly for two hours on his chosen theme: "A belief in God is totally unnecessary for moral and ethical living." We were enchanted by his logic; but could not agree with his conclusions. At the end of his address a strange thing happened. He seemed to relax. Apparently a new thought came to him. He looked at us, a group of theologians, and he said: "But I cannot compete with you. I have no hope." And he sat down sadly. Dr. Ayers had been exposed to God's table of spiritual food, but he had chosen to feed himself on plastic chips. He was starving to death.

I choose the faith where the hope is. People die when they have no hope. Christ brought hope both in life and in death. And hope becomes trust, and trust becomes character, and character is life. Character also produces right relationships. It all comes through the spirit. In this tortured world God prepares a table in the presence of our spiritual needs.

God's table is set to meet the demands of life. As we are running scared, and stumble breathless before the tent in life's desert, God quiets us, heals us, cleanses us, strengthens us and sends us on ready for the next encounter. Jesus had a word for it:

> *Come unto me all ye*
> *that labor and are*
> *heavy laden,*
> *And I will give you rest.*

Some believe in a static truth. We believe in a living, knowing, loving, acting truth: a personal, Christ-like God.

A missionary friend told me about flying out of Kabul in Afghanistan. The mountains rise abruptly around Kabul. I know, because I've been. And those Russian jets rise very slowly. I have experienced this. As my friend flew out of Kabul, there was a Russian diplomat sitting next to him. When these Russian planes fly over a mountain you are never sure they are going to make it. As the jet was struggling to get over the mountain with little room to spare, the diplomat was heard by my friend to whisper: "God help us; we are not going to make it." The missionary said, "You are a believer?" The Russian answered, "No, no, I'm a Communist. That was just a meaningless expression." But to the missionary, it sounded like a prayer; maybe it was really an unconscious prayer. Under the threat of death the prayer just burst out. The philosophy of Communism just couldn't totally drown out a deeper truth. "O God, help us." It was there in his subconscious mind. Even for a Communist there was a table in the presence of extremity. He almost accepted it.

Science and technology can get the spaceship off the launching pad and guide it to the moon; they cannot make the astronauts love each other; they cannot take care of them if reentry fails. Without God there are devastating limitations to life. By faith I face the pilgrimage. I see only a little way. The lightning flashes, I see the road. Then all is blackness, but I believe the road is still there. The next flash, I see the road again. And as I go on and on, I feel and know a presence.

By that stone in the Garden of Gethsemane, Jesus knelt at God's table in the presence of his enemies. He found peace. Some of our young men found it as they faced death in the fox holes of Viet Nam. Maybe in such extremities God will show us the path to peace. Perhaps this table could become a peace table where enemies could meet in forgiveness and establish justice.

Really, who are these enemies seeking to destroy us? Often they sneak up and destroy us, even before we know who they are. What is it that is robbing us of love? What destroys our peace of mind? What causes the burn-out where I lose the incentive for life? Do we dare look the enemy in the face? Often we accept a fake reason rather than the real reason. We blame it on so many things that are not the cause at all. Perhaps while we catch our breath under the protection of the Bedouin's tent we can pause and look back at those shadows that have been pursuing us. We are shocked to see that their faces are strangely like our own faces. Some of them are our own doubts, our own blindness, our own greed, our lack of commitment, our lack of real love, our own misreading of life. As a recent book put it, "having everything we ever wanted, we realize that it's not enough." Where does that deep gnawing hunger come from?

These fake things are trapping us, are keeping us from full life, are keeping us from digging down into the deep reservoirs of God where life breaks through, and satisfaction and peace are experienced. Paul speaks to this computer age, as he faced the spiritual enemies of his own day:

> *"I pray that your inward eyes may be illumined, so that you may know what is the hope to which he calls you, what the wealth and glory of the share he offers you among his people . . . , and how vast the resources of his power open to us who trust him.*
> (Ephesians 1:18)

This is the real table that God places before us in the presence of the real enemies of life. The table is prepared; the reservoirs of truth, power and love are open to us. The vast resources of God's inexhaustible power are available to us at any time, under any circumstances.

"He prepareth a table before me" in the face of our needs. We come to the table running scared, wounded helpless, hopeless. That's all right. That's why God prepares the table. We come to him in extremity, all torn to pieces. God gets with us because we have come to him. He quiets us down; helps us to see our problem straight. He cleanses us, heals us, strengthens us and sends us out into life again, ready for the next encounter. And the presence will be there also, if we have eyes to see.

We are fed, nourished, sustained for a purpose, not just to settle down satisfied and full; but to share this great vision of life with others. To explain it to those who are scared, broken and hopeless. To rekindle ice-bound hearts, to heal the wounded. To go and bring hope to those who struggle in the desert. To unseal the springs of life for humanity. To tell them about the vast resources of God's power open to them, open to them who trust him.

> *"He prepareth a table before us in the presence of our enemies."*

John describes the ultimate table that God has prepared:

> *And God shall wipe away all tears*
> *from their eyes;*
> *And there shall be no more death;*
> *neither sorrow, nor crying,*
> *Neither shall there be any more pain:*
> *for the former things are passed away.*
> (Revelation 21:4)

CHAPTER VII
God's Extravagance

"Thou anointest my head with oil;
my cup runneth over."
                    Psalm 23:5

Yesterday, I walked on a cold winter afternoon, but I was warmed by the brilliant sun. I thanked God that he had thought to put a stove on our planet. God's benevolent energy is always overflowing into the world about us. Even in times of darkness, discouragement and fear; in spite of the darkness, there is always "a crack in the door of darkness:" for those who have faith. God is extravagant with his sustaining care and love; it is always there. "He anointeth my head with oil; my cup runneth over."

Strangely my wounds are healed; strangely my life overflows with meaning. Joan Sauro, in a meditation in *Weavings,* suggests, "I was born connected." Through those prebirth nine months she had been sustained by the umbilical cord which connected her to her mother. Everything she had needed as a growing fetus had been supplied through that connection. Then she became aware of the spiritual cord of sustenance that had always connected her to her Heavenly Father and still met all of her deepest spiritual needs. We were "born connected" and we still are.

There is much that modern science and technology cannot do for us. They can get us off the launching pad; they can guide us to the moon. But science and technology cannot make the astronauts love each other; nor can science meet their eternal needs if reentry fails. There is that deeper supply line that we depend on. Herschel points it out: "The predicament of the child is the predicament of the parent; the predicament of a human being is the predicament of God." It comforts me to know this.

I am hit with an unresolved conflict in my daily living. I call out to God for help. I get more than I ask. The thief on the cross cried out to Jesus: "Remember me." He got back: "This day you shall be with me in paradise."

We are told that a shepherd in Palestine will stand each evening at the door of the sheepfold and examine each sheep for wounds, cuts and bruises, and bites. (There are warble flies, bot flies, heel flies, nose flies, deer flies, black flies, green flies, mosquitoes, gnats.) Such is life, so many things attack us. The shepherd will gently rub into these wounds a healing ointment. Perhaps the wound is on the head; and he anoints the head with oil. Over and over again my hurts and wounds have been healed: Peace has been restored; hope has dawned again; health has returned. If this were not true, by this time, I would be wrapped from head to toe in the bandages of my own sufferings.

But some might say, "We just got well! We just got over it." That is true. God has so ordered the universe; God has so structured human nature. But we have felt something more, especially as we have looked back upon life: A love and a tenderness (a warm experience in the subconscious), a personal concern for our needs. "Like as a Father pitieth his children . . ." "Not even a bird falleth to the ground . . ." "I am healed, I am launched again into life." He anointeth my head with oil."

God has maintained a heavy bank account of love and care in the name of each of us. Sadly, we have failed to draw on our account. Thornton Wilder in his book, *The Eighth Day*, tells about a man riding a slow train up the Andes. At a little Andean village a mother and seven children crowded into his tiny compartment. The father had just been killed in a mining accident. The oldest daughter was trying to comfort her mother and the children. But the mother continued to wail: "Tell them we have nothing to live for — tell them we have nothing to live for."

Then some fool comes along (God's fool) and declares: "He anointeth my head with oil; my cup runneth over." "Fear not little flock; it is your Father's good pleasure to give you the kingdom (Luke 12:32)." "Be of good cheer; I have overcome the world (John 16:33)." "God loves you — particularly you." And the little family begins to catch a glimpse of the possibility of life yet ahead of them.

George Buttrick once wrote that we are walking across the crust of hell, and the crust is thin. When we look at life we see some truth in this. But we can listen more deeply and hear the concerned agony of God. We can see Christ in his resurrection beckoning to us. When fear, guilt, death are so "in," in our secular culture; God, forgiveness, love are just as much "in," in our faith culture.

Why do we doubt our beliefs and believe our doubts? It is far better to doubt our doubts and believe our beliefs. When we dare to trust our beliefs, we hear some strange echoes from the eternal:

> *"Who forgiveth all thine iniquities,*
> *Who healeth all thy diseases,*
> *Who redeemeth thy life from destruction,*
> *Who crowneth thee with loving kindness*
> *and tender mercies."*
> (Psalm 103:3-4)

An old Rabbi was on his death bed and he whispered: "God won't ask me why I wasn't Moses; he will ask me why I was not myself." He has called me to be me. I must find out who that me is. What does God have in mind for me?

Life can be rough on us. Like sheep we go out into the world every day to graze. It's a rough world. And at times we make it rough for others. Sometimes it is like a person trying to run up an escalator that is coming down. It's hard to get ahead. At times we are caught in a one-way street going the wrong direction, and we are blocked. Why does all this happen to us?

Jean-Paul Satre says, "We are condemned to be free;" and that is rough. We have to make decisions; we have to make our own way and we bump into other people who are trying to make their own way. God does not put us in a strait-jacket. He gives us freedom and therefore we are responsible. Freedom is wonderful, but freedom is costly. This is not a world of happy stories about happy people who have happy problems. No, but it is a world that grows people, when they are sensitive to God — and Christ is the key. He is the one who heals our wounds and guides us in the way.

At times there is mass wandering because of conformity to the wrong peer group. There was a recent news story of a sheep stampede in Switzerland. A thousand sheep ($42,000 worth of sheep) stampeded over a high cliff into the valley below. There was nothing left but a tangled mess of broken bodies at the base of the cliff. How did it start? Perhaps a small rockslide, maybe some wild animal. It started; each sheep following blindly the sheep ahead of him, not seeing the end result of such a race. Now the sheep could not stop if they wanted to. The pressure of the sheep racing behind them prevented them from turning back. It was like a living stream of death; it flowed like a waterfall over the precipice. Perhaps the real cause was fear; no vision, no understanding. They were caught, like some of us, in the evil flow of life that became the flow of death; and after a certain point could not be stopped. But Christ is the kind of shepherd who even after the panic button has been pushed, can make something out of the mess of broken lives at the foot of the cliff. I have seen many broken lives restored. Christ doesn't give up on us. I am beginning to understand the meaning of grace — God's power in my life to produce a new nature.

Sometimes we are caught in a situation we can't handle; it won't work out. Perhaps it's alcohol or drugs, or sex, or greed, or fear or guilt. Desperate, we attack it with all our strength and fail. Exhausted, we cry out to God for help. We feel a new assurance. We make progress. We are thrown back. But a strange inner drive, that seems to come from beyond ourselves, keeps us at it. We won't give up; something won't let us give up. We figure to find a more satisfying adjustment to things, to people and to ourselves. People begin to respond to us. People change, situations change, I change. Life begins to be ordered on a higher level, from a deeper center. God kept us on our feet, going forward, until we saw "the crack in the door of darkness." We begin to understand our freedom, our cross, our victory. This is God's grace in action — "My cup runneth over."

We have a simple illustration: A mother's world has gone sour. It is more than she can handle. Her home is going to pieces. She cries out to God for help. She starts a new quest in Bible reading — letting it speak to her problem. She begins a new prayer program where she thinks with God about her real problems. She examines herself and her relationships with her family. She began to see that love had to be practiced and that someone had to start. She couldn't put it off until other members of the family acted.

She was moved to plunge headlong into a new pattern of life. The next morning, instead of fussing at everybody, she amazed her husband by asking: "Cup of coffee, dear? Your majesty, would you like your breakfast in bed?" He flipped! But he reacted to a new attitude, with a fresh attitude of his own.

She went to her son's room. She kissed him. (There had been little affection between them.) She said, "Bob, darling." He answered, "Darling?" She came back, "Yes, I love you, Bob."

That day there were many surprises and laughter. Such things as, "Let me do it." The spirit caught in the whole family. There was a revolution in that home. A revolution began to take hold of the neighborhood.

The mother felt a new joy, a new confidence. Amazing grace! He anointeth my head with the oil of peace. My cup of joy runneth over into the lives of others.

Sadly, there is another side of the coin. If we insist we can make every day a deadly burden. In his book, *Under His Own Signature,* Leslie Weatherhead tells of visiting a home which was more like a tomb than a house, the persons living there were more dead than alive. "No light in their eyes, no joy in their voices." Weatherhead continued, "They reminded me of dull, heavy oxen plowing a muddy field uphill on a rainy day." This is where some people come out. God does not intend it so. When we deny God, we refuse his blessings.

This is a searching question: What if God gave us only the same amount of time and attention we give to him? The more my mind is open to God the more blessings I receive. Again and again in our lives God has broken in, the direction of our lives has been turned, we have been prevented from the precipice.

At times our problems are tasks that God has assigned to us. Problems can be a mission: a family problem, a business problem, a community problem. This can be a call. But some of us are 4F Christians. Life is full of divine assignments. In spite of his sufferings, Christ's cup of joy overflowed. Because of life's involvements, my cup overflows.

General Booth of the Salvation Army, as an old man in the hospital, discovered he was going blind. He said, to his son, Bramwell: "You mean I am going blind." His son answered, "I am afraid that is true." "You mean I will never see your face again?" Bramwell answered, "Not in this world." The old man reached his hand across the bed and said, "Bramwell, I have done what I could for God and the people with my eyes. Now I shall do what I can for God and the people without my eyes." Now that is the grace of God made possible by faith. God is always at the other end of our faith.

Look at Moses. He was a fugitive from a collapsed life in Egypt. He was caught up in an encounter with God on the back side of the desert. He was launched again in a dangerous mission freeing his people from slavery. The impossible demands of his mission forced him into a deep dependence on God. He was sustained in his mission. At the end of the journey he is alone as his people march on into the Promised Land. But he has found his peace in the presence of God. God and fulfillment are at the end of the journey of faith.

Someone suggests a frightening thought:

If God Should Go On Strike
How good it is that God above has
    never gone on strike
Because he was not treated fair in
    things he didn't like.
If only once he'd given up and said,
    "That's it, I'm through,
"I've had enough of thee on earth,
    so this is what I'll do.

"I'll give my orders to the sun, cut
    off the heat supply.
And to the moon give no more light
    and run the oceans dry.
Then just to make things really tough
    and put the pressure on,
Turn off the vital oxygen till every
    breath is gone."

You know he would be justified, if
    fairness were the game.
For no one has been more abused
    or met with more disdain
Than God, and yet he carries on,
    supplying you and me
With all the favors of his grace, and
    everything for free . . . .
        — Author unknown

But God doesn't go on strike, just the opposite. C. S. Lewis describes his Christian experience in his book titled *Surprised by Joy*. Why should we be so surprised by joy? It is God's plan for us where we are faithful. Evelyn Underhill shames our lack of faith, "(God) rides upon the floods. It is because of our limitations that we seem only to receive him in trickles." The fact is that in that final day:

"The morning stars
Shall sing together;
And all the sons of men
Shall shout with joy."

Sometimes in experiences of prayer it is given to us to know in flashes of insight the wonders of God present within our lives. Power surges through the soul, clearness and vision possess the mind, the vistas of the future open up, the paths, once clouded, are seen straight and clear. Walls and fences disappear, there is no real threat anywhere in the universe. We are free; life is seen in the new dimension, horizons stretch out toward the dawning visibility of the city of God.

My cup runneth over —
In deep and moving experiences of worship.

My cup runneth over —
In prayer and adoration.

My cup runneth over —
In joyous service and love.

My cup runneth over —
In sharing and in healing.

My cup runneth over —
In seeing, in feeling, and in living.

My cup runneth over —
In Christ, in the Holy Spirit, and in God.

This is life eternal. This is God's extravagance.

CHAPTER VIII
The Final Dimensions Of Life

> *"Surely goodness and mercy*
> *Shall follow me all the days of my life:*
> *And I will dwell in the house of*
> *The Lord forever."*
>
> Psalm 23:6

What a climax: "Goodness and mercy all the days of my life;" and "dwell in the house of the Lord, forever." For the Christian, that is life's fulfillment.

But so few of us really grasp the full meaning of life. The governor of Tennessee tells about a letter from a prisoner recently received:

> *"Dear Governor,*
> *I want to talk with you about my future.*
> *I am o be electrocuted on Friday,*
> *And here it is Wednesday.*
>
> *Your friend —*

One of us might address God:

> *O God,*
> *I want to talk to you about my future.*
> *I am going to run out of life one of these days and here I am 80 years old.*
>
> *Your friend —*

But here we are, all mixed up as to life's real meaning:

> *"In a day of illusions*
> *And utter confusions*
> *Upon our delusions*
> *We base our conclusions."*

God help us. We try to air-condition hell, instead of finding the true meaning of life. Really, what is the score? Leslie

Weatherhead gives us a parable: There is an imaginary ship cruising in mid-ocean. The captain called the passengers together and announced:

> *"We are not going to put into port. We have food; we have music. We will continue our cruise with dancing and singing until our fuel is exhausted, and then sink the ship."*

How stupid can you get? But many of us are doing just that. We are preoccupied with the present moment — with our money-making and our dancing. We have no awareness of destiny. Without thinking, we have made up our minds to ride the ship until the fuel runs out, and let her sink. Thomas Merton is right, "Our problem is desire — not great desire, but low desire." Life has no grand mystique. Youth is caught up in "frenzied pleasure-seeking." Too many are filling their emptiness with alcohol, drugs and careless sex.

And the result? Emil Brunner answers, "All (these) paths lead into the grave. This is the fearful geography of life." Paul Tillich goes a step farther, "Who can look at this picture? Only those who look at another picture beyond this picture." And that picture is the picture of God's love on the cross, and the picture of death defeated by the resurrection.

We can't accept the theme of a recent author: "The deepening twilight moves across the lovely sweep of the earth. This and only this is all, there is no more." No! We have a choice. "We must make up our minds," suggests Rufus Jones. "Are we going to live in a one-story universe or a two-story universe?" Does not the ultimate end of life give meaning to the present? As Bob Dylan sings it: "He not busy being born is busy dying."

There is the story about a submarine, badly damaged by a depth charge, and lying on the bottom of the ocean. In trying to surface the craft, the captain organized two groups: one, to work night and day on surfacing; two, to carry on life, meantime, food, recreation and housekeeping. The second group says to group number one, "Why waste time trying to surface? This is life. You are missing out on it." The captain had to speak, "Up there is true life. We live here, temporarily, so we can live there, permanently." The captain speaks to us: "Life, real life, is up there where God is." That is the goal; this is only temporary.

Let's get our bearings. We take soundings. How deep is our ocean? Where is our port? What is really up there on the surface with God? The soul's radar picks up a dim message:

> *"Surely goodness and mercy*
> *Shall follow me all the days of my life,*
> *And I shall dwell*
> *in the house of the Lord forever."*

Our radar constantly searches all horizons. There is a persistent blip. It may be blurred, but it is there. It won't go away. It beckons. By faith we follow. God doesn't spell it out too easily. Life can be fearful. But I won't give up. I feel in my bones the expectation of some great thing: "The house of the Lord, forever."

Intelligent as we are, it is so easy for us human beings to get fatally trapped. Just the other day, an insect flew through my study window. I said you won't like this. You will be trapped away from the sun, the flowers and nature. Confidently (by his actions), the insect answered back: "You are wrong. It's bright and warm in here, and I smell something intriguing. I can go back when I wish." He stayed. The next morning he was dead. Should not several million years of evolution have carried us a little further along the road of wise action?

Harold Bosley told of a little girl visiting in the home of friends. She was crying like her heart would break. When her hostess asked, "Honey, are you homesick?" She whimpered, "No, ma'am, I'm here sick." In our holding on to a one dimensional world, we are "here sick," hungry for the full expression of our powers, hungry to know that we are in a continuing stream of life, that leads somewhere.

Now let's move to the eternal reality: "the goodness and mercy;" "the house of the Lord forever." This life is tied to the next life; the next life is tied to this life. A young mother advises her growing child: "Live each day in an awareness of your relationship to a real God, who knows you and is working with you. Seek in everything to obey him, and seek to accomplish what he calls you to." Our obedience to God and our support from God is practical and continuous. It is lived out in personal life, in work and in leisure, in corporate and professional life, and most of all in all relationships with others.

Just now I am having counseling sessions with a very depressed woman in our church. She is worrying and afraid; she is making herself physically sick. She is in and out of the hospital and under partial psychiatric care. I have reminded her that Jesus said, "My peace I leave with you. My peace I give unto you. Not as the world giveth give I unto you, let not your heart be troubled neither let it be afraid (John 14:27)." I have tried to help her receive this gift of peace as a sheer gift from Christ. Just breathe in this quiet mysterious gift of peace. Just receive it and begin thanking God for it every moment you receive it until it becomes a life habit of trust and joy, and depression fades away. I saw her yesterday and I could see the depression fading and the lines of trust and peace beginning to be written into her face.

We learn to turn threats and fears, sickness and problems over to him. We feel the burden lifted. We realize God is working at it, that he knows the situation, that he can handle it, that he will handle it. A new trust has been born in our subconscious minds. And we move toward wholeness. And we are deeply assured that he can even handle death; and there will be a beautiful sunrise in a totally new universe of life. As one of my members spoke to me on his death-bed, "In my funeral tell them that I said: 'My life has had just enough clouds to make a beautiful sunset.' " "Goodness and mercy" in spite of tragedy; always help at the pressure-points of life. We live each day in this relaxed strength of trust, assurance and thankfulness. And we know down deep that everything is all right. And we expect more and more until the task is done, and our work is over, and he calls us home. After the "goodness and mercy," the "house of the Lord forever."

All our lives we've been operating in the house of the Lord. My father is gone, but he is in God. I am alive, but I am in God. We are both alive in God at different levels of experience. God is not condoning all our selfishness and stubbornness, but he is forgiving as we repent. If I am obeying as I understand and seeking to grow, God is forgiving things I honestly miss and instructing me in my failures. The goodness and the mercy follow me. This goes on into the eternal.

Now where does faith come in? Commitment which is made possible through trust opens the door to realized experience and assurance. Jesus asked, "When the Son of Man cometh, will he find faith on earth?" If not we are lost; in faith we see the way, a step at a time. God draws us out, little by little. He gives us footprints in the distance, a lantern in the darkness, a door set open before us. God wants us to be born a little every day. This is exploring the goodness and the mercy. We share the goodness and the mercy all the days of our lives, period! And then by the grace of God we leap over the wall — "The house of the Lord forever." When one discovers the goodness and the mercy, he will come face to face with the forever. When we are headed toward the kingdom of God, we can see it.

As George Santayana reminded us: "Whoever it was who searched the heavens with a telescope and found no God would not have found the human mind if he had searched the human brain with a microscope." But God is there — the goodness and the mercy — and you see him by faith.

Once flying back over the Alps from Yugoslavia to Frankfort, Germany, our plane felt its way down cloud canyons through "mystical halls of air." Guided by instruments, piercing misty curtain after misty curtain, we came at last safely to our destination. Guided through life by faith, piercing curtains, coming from the unkonwn to the known, from the unseen to the seen, through joys and through sorrows, overshadowed by the goodness and mercy, we come at last through the final curtain and burst in upon eternal day. The sun rises never to set again. The Psalmist had lived under the goodness and the mercy all the days of his life. But then he ran out of days; he ran head-on into a wall, the end of things. Then by the power of God, he leaps over the wall and takes up life again on the other side: "and I shall dwell in the house of the Lord, forever." This is the total experience of life.

We are not to be afraid of death. Here the "walls" and the "ceilings" of life melt away, the horizons are pushed back, the wonderful light engulfs everything; and we are in God's house. Paul Scherer says it: "Death is no longer the end; God is the end!" It all looks different when we look at God, and not at death. His goodness and mercy flows from this life into the next life. With God the limits are removed — "And I shall dwell in the house of the Lord forever."

Our prioneer fathers who traveled west had nothing to go on except the tales of those survivors who had gone before. It was enough. They dared to go, discovering and building as they went, and behold, a new world was born.

The deep realities are seen by persons of faith. An old Rabbi was dying. His friends were listening: "I can see no walls, no ceiling. I can only see the life of everything and God creating everything and making everything live." "There is always a great city at the end of a great highway." We are always graduating. First from kindergarten to grammar school, then from grammar school to junior high, and junior to senior high, then we are graduated to college. From college we graduate into life and our work, from work we finally retire into a more relaxed base of creativity. From retirement we graduate into heaven (if we love and trust the Giver of Life).

But so many of us have lost respect for life, have sold it cheap, have thrown it away, because we have no clear vision of our ultimate destiny at the end of the road. C. S. Lewis speaks to us sharply: "Only since Christians have ceased to think of the other world have they become so ineffective in this." Only by seeing life whole with a great faith can we "fuel the engine for dynamic Christian action and mission in the world." "The Christian is one whose death is already behind him." He knows it and always lives in expectation of the next step and the next great experience.

What do people really live for? —

To know the roots of knowledge —
To heal the hearts of men —
To find the source of being —
To discover the foundations of life's meaning —
To pierce the mystery of life —
To hear the beginning and the end of great music —
To glimpse the city of God —
To explore the majesty of creation —
To grasp the day of peace —
To see the fulfillment of love —

Can you accomplish all this in 80 years of physical life? No! There is another chapter for which this chapter is being written.

"Christ has brought life and immortality to light." One who has memory and hope, must have perspective or he dies. What is the whole picture? Now walk with me by faith and we shall see:

We cross the plains,
We scale the hills.

The mountain wall looms dark; impassable,
But then, a piercing shaft of light at sunset,
A pass unseen before,
Suggest a land of glorious brightness!

A Trail,
Some drops of blood and sweat,
A cross, so lovely, standing by —
Up, up; and in the pass an empty tomb!

Now, unafraid to tread
Where Christ has led,
We step at last,
From night to day!

It's not a bribe — "It's just where the road leads to."

Roy Smith draws the final picture:

The Psalmist is old
The curtain is being drawn
The lights are going down
The sheepfold is closed
The sheep are asleep
And across the ages
A song of hope is heard:

The Lord is my shepherd
The green pastures and the still waters
The paths of Righteousness
He restoreth my soul
The Valley of the Shadow
Thou art with me
Thy table before me
My cup runneth over
The goodness and mercy
The House of the Lord, Forever.

Amen

CHAPTER IX
The Shepherd God Comes To Earth

"So the Word became flesh; he came to dwell among us."
John 1:14

When John writes "Logos" or "Word" in the first chapter of his gospel he means Christ. So we translate it that way:

"When all things began, the Christ already was. The Christ dwelt with God, and what God was, the Christ was. The Christ then, was with God at the beginning, and through him all things came to be .... All that came to be was alive with his life." (John 1:1-4)

The Eternal Shepherd God "became flesh; and came to dwell among us." He came in the form of Christ so that we could see him, hear him, touch him and be touched by him. That was a dark day in history but the Light broke through.

This is a dark day in history, as Glen Lanier writes:

Write these things down, and tell it through the land.
"No hope remains; there is no guilding hand.
The Word is dead — the prophets all have died,
Men make mockery of the Crucified.

All truth is turned to falsehood; faith to doubt,
and all the lighted candles are blown out . . ."

Yet on the dark horizon still I see,
A cross-framed form still calling, 'Look to me.' "

In the darkest days the Shepherd God is still with us, here on earth, where the problems are.

Some years ago a young man from my church came home from his first year at college for the Christmas holidays. He came to see me and asked one question: "Pastor, I believe in God, but where does Christ come in?" This chapter seeks to answer that question.

In Christ God is revealing himself to humanity in technicolor. He is interpreting himself for us in the teachings, the spirit and life of Jesus. The Shepherd God is saying to us today: "I sent my Spirit of Love into your world and you crucified him; yet, he still loves you, and it is time you responded to that love." Christ is a far more total revelation of the reality of enduring life than any of us have fully imagined. "I am the way, the truth, and the life (John 14:6)."

In other world religions, man is desperately seeking God. In Christ, God is seeking man, pursuing him in love. Dr. C. A. Coulson, head of the department of higher mathematics at Oxford University, an outstanding world physicist, was also a great Christian. I was having tea with him once in a little London tea room. He said a strange thing for an outstanding physicist: "When I get to heaven, the first thing I'm going to do is look up someone from another planet and I am going to ask them, 'How did God come to your planet redemptively? And what did you do about it? — We crucified ours.'" Dr. Coulson has since gone to be with God, and now he knows.

His statement helps to clarify my own understanding of Christ. If there are other planets where life has advanced to the level of ours, in "the fullness of time" God would have sent his Eternal Spirit to be born in one of them in order to reveal to the people of that planet what God is like in their own terms. He would live out his life there suffering everything they had to suffer, revealing his Spirit and the ways of life abundant and the reality of life eternal. God would do that for any planet where he has children and that's what he did for the planet Earth when he came in Christ. So now we know what God is like as far as human beings can grasp infinity, and we know what we are called to be. That is where Christ comes in.

To put it another way, we look at a great power line stretching across the country and realize it might be carrying as much as 400,000 volts. We know that if we ran this into our homes, it would kill us all. For this reason, every town has a transformer station where this voltage is cut down to 110 volts before it is run into our homes, and we use it without danger. When we realize that all the nuclear energy in all the billions of suns in the universe is an expression of God's unbelievable energy, then we see why God had to transform his direct approach and come to us in one of us, Jesus of Nazareth. In Christ we see all that man can comprehend of the nature of God. But there is more — so much more:

> *"Eye hath not seen,*
> *Nor ear heard; neither hath it*
> *entered into the heart of man*
> *the things that God hath prepared*
> *for them that love him."*
> (1 Corinthians 2:9)

Christ is God holding a light so that humanity might see eternal things in a world of darkness. God's love invaded our world in Jesus Christ.

I believe there are six specific reasons why God gave us Christ; why the Shepherd God became incarnate:

One: God saw that something had to be done about humankind's hopeless lostness, so he gave us Christ. In Asheville, North Carolina, I was working with a group of psychiatrists. One night at dinner one of the doctors sitting next to me said: "Pastor, there was a woman in my office this morning so burdened with guilt she wanted to destroy herself. I told her, 'Forget it! No good God wants to send one of his children to hell.' " I surprised him by answering, "You are right, Doctor. God is not in the business of sending his children to hell. He is in the business of getting them out of hell — the hells they put themselves into. And Christ on a cross is the extremity to which God goes to rescue his children from their lostness."

Another psychiatrist sent me one of his patients whose problems seemed to go beyond the usual psychological treatment. I can see her as she sat across from my desk, wringing her hands in agony. She was crying out: "I can't trust God! I can't trust God!" I was praying inwardly and I remembered that she had some background in the Christian faith so I said: "God is not mad at you. He is worried about you. He sees that one of his children is all worried and confused and he wants to help you."

Then I was helped further in this interview. I was inwardly praying all the time. I asked her: "If you had lived in Galilee, and had followed Jesus in one of his days of teaching and healing. If you had seen him take the little children in his arms, and heal all kinds of sickness; if you had heard him speak and listened to him pray; if you had felt his love and compassion for all the people, would you have trusted him? Would you have thought, 'He'll just pick me up and let me down?' Or would you have felt, 'Here is someone whose love is genuine — I can believe in him; I can trust him?' Could you have trusted Jesus?"

My friend thought for a moment and answered: "Yes, I think I could have trusted Jesus." Then I asked, "Well, if you could have trusted Jesus, might you not trust God, the Father, who is back of Jesus, who gave us Jesus, who reveals his love in Jesus?" Again she hesitated thoughtfully. A little light of recognition came into her eyes. I prayed and asked her to pray aloud. She was much more at peace. She left, but she had begun to see God in Christ. Without Christ, she might never have found her way out of lostness to whole life again. That's where Christ comes in.

Two: God saw that something had to be done about our understanding of truth, so he gave us Christ. We live in a world of confused values. We are not at all sure what is real. We call evil things good, and good things bad. What is everlastingly real?

After having coached track and taught history at the Tome School in Maryland, I had a deep compulsion that I should stop coaching (which I loved), go to seminary and get ready to preach. I didn't want to. But I obeyed. Thank God. It has been a wonderful life.

When I reached seminary and was introduced to philosophical religion, I began to wonder about the simple faith I had had since my conversion at 11 years of age. I could see that my professors knew more than I did. But they didn't seem to feel the reality and the presence of God as I did. I wondered if my experience of Christ was real.

I didn't doubt for one minute that God was calling me to preach. The question was, what was true, what could I preach? You can't preach it unless you are convinced in your own soul, it is true. What was true? I struggled with intellectual faith problems for three months. It was an awful struggle. What was true? What could I preach in all honesty?

Then at three o'clock one morning, I was on my knees in a cold dark room alone and hopeless in my struggle. Suddenly, out of that cold darkness there came a message. It was clearly spoken. The words were not spoken outside me, but inside me, but they were explicit: "If there be a God, all he wants you to do is to find out what is true, and give your life to that." God picked me up where I was and started me on the path back to reality. I didn't have to believe anything that was false. I just had to discover what was true and give my life that. That made sense. I was at peace. I got up, went back to bed and slept until morning.

I awoke not in darkness, but in a new light. All I had to do was to find out what was true, and preach that, and God would help me. It was a whole new world and I was on my quest. I started with my New Testament, looking at Christ. A truth came to me. If I could just be more like him, that would be life. I looked at my world. We had problems. Every generation has problems. We are here to solve the problems of the world. I saw that if the leaders and the people of my world would just approach problems in Christ's spirit we would begin to work out those problems. I was sure; I could preach it.

The Holy Spirit led me deeper and deeper in my quest. I saw that this Jesus was not a temporary thing. He was not just a good man helping people in one moment of time. There was something beyond this earth here. I could see something eternal from the center of the universe, something powerful from the heart of creation. I could see God rising to the surface of life in Jesus and becoming visible for our sakes. I could see God in Christ. I could preach that. It was true; I knew it was true. Through the next three months I found my way back to faith, to certainty. I had found my way back to God through Jesus. I understood truth and ultimate reality. That's where Christ comes in.

Three: God knew that something had to be done about humanity's inability to cope with life, so he gave us Christ. We are not handling life so well. We are failing in many areas. My son was teaching at Fuller Seminary in Pasadena, California. A young doctor came to him for help. The doctor said, "Tuttle, I've got a good practice. I've got more money than I need. I've got three cars, a beautiful home here and a house at the beach. I have a fast boat. I have a wonderful wife and three beautiful children. I have everything I ever wanted. Why do I want to blow my brains out?"

My son answered, "Doctor, you have lived your life. You have accomplished all your goals. You are through. There is nothing else to gain. So I guess you just have to blow it."

And then, quickly, my son added. "But wait a minute. Before you blow it, I dare you to try one more thing. Get yourself and material things out of the center of your life. Start living for God instead of yourself. Turn your home, your practice, your wealth over to him. Start serving Christ in all that you do. There will be a difference, I promise you. You will do more than just fix your patients up medically. You will care for them as persons. You will heal both body and soul. You will give them hope and something to live for. You will see a look of gratitude and new life deep in their eyes. You will be glad. You can't get enough of it. Your whole world will be different for you and your family. You won't think about wanting to blow your brains out again. Christ will be your eternal friend with whom you work."

The young doctor got the message. It was a new world!

I heard Dr. McKay, president of Princeton Seminary, tell of an experience when he was a missionary in the jungles of Brazil. A member of a bank robbery gang was converted. It was obvious that he had to give up his profession. He was growing as a Christian, but after a few months the old gang showed up at his little cottage on the edge of the jungle. They needed him for just one more job. John refused them. They continued to persuade as John's wife stood on the porch watching. John was holding out bravely until the old gang began to shame him. "John, you are yellow. You are a coward; you can't take it anymore." His wife saw his face turn red, the veins in his neck bulge out, his fists clinch. She knew that they were getting to him. In her terrible fear that he would give in, she called out, "Remember Christ, John; remember Christ!"

She saw his fists relax. His face regained its natural color. The veins in his neck became normal. And John took it. Under the sway of Christ, John took it!

That's where Christ comes in. He enables us to cope, to handle life. He forgives us; he sustains us.

Four: God knew that something had to be done about our inability to love, so he gave us Christ. Look at the hate, the violence, the fighting, the terrorism in the world. Look at the lack of deep love between husband and wife. We tremble when we read about the abuse of children. We feel the tension between management and the work force. Why do we live adversely instead of cooperatively?

God sent Christ to love us and show us how much God loves us. When we know that we are loved, it makes it easier to love each other. When Christ touched sick persons here on earth they knew that they were loved and they knew that God loved them, and they were healed. It is still possible, in spirit, to reach out and touch the hem of his garments and be touched by him, and be healed.

Once I had an alcoholic newspaper man in my church. He was converted and became a beautiful Christian. His paper told of a poor woman with eight children in our town who was being turned off welfare. He knew that she would suffer and that those children would suffer. He asked his wife to go with him to see the woman. They went and they told her that they loved her, that they would help her and the children. The desperate woman regained her hope. That's where Christ comes in — teaching us to love and to care. We can't have the blessing of Christ unless we are obedient to the Spirit of Christ. When I know that I am loved, I can love everybody.

Five: God knew that something had to be done about our sins, and he gave us Christ. I have sinned, you have sinned. We have all fallen short of the goodness of Christ. We live under a heavy burden of guilt. All of us need to be forgiven again and again. We need to know that we are forgiven.

We live in a universe of judgment. God made it so. God told Amos, "With a plumb line will I judge my people (Amos 7:8)." If a building is not built on the square it falls. If a business is not built on honesty it fails. If a home is not built on faithfulness it falls. If a nation is not founded on righteousness it falls. We know where we stand with God, but so often we fall short. Into this world of judgment God sent Christ to forgive our sins, to die for our sins, and to let us know we are forgiven when we repent.

The cross is a dilemma. Why did a good God let Jesus suffer and die on a cross? God knew that Jesus wanted, more than anything in the world, to redeem humankind. God knew that it would take the death of Jesus on a cross, and then the resurrection, to grasp and hold the mind of the human race. This was the battle fought out that terrible night in the garden, kneeling by a stone. When Jesus saw this he was at peace. To put it simply:

> *There is Hope in the Cross —*
> *Hope for me!*
> *God's head bowed down —*
> *God's arms outstretched —*
> *God's heart accepting me —*
> *Even me!*

I know that Christ has forgiven me — I am free!

Even though she had intellectual problems with theology, my sister was a beautiful Christian. As a college professor she loved her students and lifted them in spirit. She gave away a large percentage of her income. All by herself she built a church for a small village in India. On her death bed she was still worried about her theological problems. But just before she died, she said to my younger sister: "I can't understand it all, but somehow I know that Christ makes the difference." And she died in peace. That's where Christ comes in.

Six: God knew that something had to be done about death, so he gave us Christ and the resurrection. The resurrection enables us to see beyond death with assurance. It is said that in America we are more afraid of death than anywhere in the world. Why? Because we are living for money and for pleasure. We have forgotten God. When I faced possible death by scarlet fever as a child, I knew I could not handle it without God. This awful fear set me on a quest after God. I found him; or he found me. I have lived with assurance ever since.

Charles Allen says that there is not an emptier place in the world than a Christian cemetery. There is nobody there, all the inhabitants have gone to heaven. Is our hope of heaven bright? John Wesley was asked: "Mr. Wesley, what would you do if you knew you were going to die tonight?" It is said that he answered: "I would do exactly as I had planned. I would ride on to Tewksbury, for I have an appointment to preach there tonight. After the services I would go home with Brother and Sister Brown, for they are expecting me. We would sit around the fire in conversation, we would read scripture and have prayer. At 10 o'clock I would retire to my room, commend my soul to God, go fast asleep and wake up in Glory."

After the crucifixion the disciples were scared to death. Their master was dead; they were hiding. But something happened on that third day. There was the resurrection. Their master came back. They saw him; they talked with him. He said to them: "I go to prepare a place for you, that where I am, there you shall be also. Because I live, ye too shall live."

They weren't afraid anymore. When the authorities commanded them not to preach anymore in the name of Jesus, they answered: "Shall we obey man, or obey God?" They went right on preaching and healing, at the risk of their lives. They weren't afraid of death anymore. They went all the way to hostile Rome sharing this new movement of love and life in the heart of the world. They were children of the resurrection. And so are we! "Be not afraid," he said, "I have overcome the world." Christians should have no apology for their faith. It is everlasting truth. "Be not afraid," nothing can harm you, not really. "And I will be with you to the end of the world," he said.

This is where Christ comes in!

Do we belong to him or do we not? If you have caught a glimpse of Christ — his love, his compassion, his goodness — and you don't like him, you don't want him disturbing your selfish lifestyle, you want nothing to do with him, you are doomed, you are damned. You have closed the door of life upon yourself. You are outside. Lost! Alone!

On the other hand, if you glimpse this Christ and you love him, you yearn to be like him, you hunger for him, you give your life to him, holding nothing back. Then you are saved both for this life and the next life by his power and mercy. And you keep growing in his spirit by his power as long as you live. And in the end he takes you home. This is Christian assurance. I am not scared anymore.

Perhaps we are tired of our lostness. We are now ready to receive him. "To them that received him, to them gave he power to become the sons and daughters of God (John 1:12)." To surrender to Christ, is to be captured by life. For in him:

Our sins are forgiven,
Our release is secured,
Our peace is given,
Our eternal life is assured.
And we become a part of
His redeeming, loving, caring force
At work in the world.

Listen! "And there is therefore now no condemnation to them that are in Christ Jesus, who walk not after the flesh but after the spirit (Romans 8:1)."

The Shepherd God, incarnate, has saved us. We are now beyond the valley of the shadow.

"I heard Christ call
'Come follow,' that was all.
My gold grew dim,
My heart went out to him,
I arose and followed,
That was all.
Who would not follow
If he heard Christ call?"

www.ingramcontent.com/pod-product-compliance
Lightning Source LLC
Chambersburg PA
CBHW060848050426
42453CB00008B/883